Understanding
CBDC

Money and Blockchain.

A critical approach to the greatest revolution since the invention of the printing press, or the dystopia that will change the world as we know it.

What they are, how they will work, the social and economic implications and how they will forever change the monetary system as we know it.

ISBN: 9788411742610

Copyright: © Martin Mendo Antunez, 2023
understandingcbdc@proton.me

Printing and editorial: BoD – Books on Demand
info@bod.com.es - www.bod.com.es
Printed in Germany

Dedicated to my wife Silvia and my son Xabier.

May 2023.

INDEX.

LEGAL NOTICE.

Prologue.

Motivated by my professional curiosity, I decided to learn about the technical workings of bitcoin and its blockchain.

To understand the technical basis, I had to understand the economic and monetary concepts mentioned in the white paper that defines bitcoin, and then I discovered what was for me a whole new world; the economic, financial, monetary and banking systems, which usually go unnoticed by most ordinary citizens, entering a gray area of unknowing, which is not accidental, and whose apparent complexity effectively discourages almost everyone from learning about these much-needed subjects, which, surprisingly, are not mandatory at all levels of education.

Since then, I have started a new hobby, learning what money is and how it works, finance, banking, understanding the financial terminology that is skillfully used by the disinformation media to keep the population ignorant about these issues, and finally understanding the connection between financiers, governments and politicians of all colors and in all countries of the world.

One of the challenges of this book is to adapt the content it analyzes for people with different knowledge bases.

An ordinary person who only receives information from the mass disinformation media with a very basic knowledge, supported by topics that we have been told since childhood, that we read in the press or see on television, might find the exposition of this book quite dense, difficult or even too "alternative".

However, a reader with a greater knowledge base, either by hobby or profession, and who is familiar with economic and financial terminology, may find the book too basic and, in its attempt to explain complex concepts in a simple way, perhaps not entirely rigorous in explaining those concepts.

The author's main goal is to provide the basic knowledge that every person should have about money, CBDC, the monetary system, and the economy of the first group; although I hope that many readers who are halfway between the two groups described will find this text an incentive to continue learning.

You may find some statements and concepts in this book so different from what we take for granted, so shocking, and perhaps so counter-intuitive, that you may find it hard to believe that they are true.

I will try to provide references where necessary, but if you find a subjective opinion of the author, I encourage you to delve into it and find out for yourself how you can expand your knowledge in this subject.

The ultimate goal of this book is to stimulate your curiosity to understand not only the new CBDC currencies, but also money, the workings of the monetary system, finance and the economy that move our world, to know the real meaning of the terms used, for which you can consult the glossary at the end of the book, and above all, to encourage you to continue learning, to be able to educate our children and our family on these subjects, since they are deliberately omitted in education plans.

Delving into the discovery of this world of finance and economics has been a healthy shock that has changed the way I see the world.

I hope you will enjoy discovering what is usually hidden or disguised with a language of euphemisms and technical terms for the initiated only, whose purpose is usually to mask the real meaning

.

CHAPTER 2.

Introduction to CBDCs.

What they are and why they are being developed.

If you have started reading this book, you have probably already heard or read something about the new digital currencies being prepared by virtually all the Central Banks in the world, some already in the testing phase, and others, such as in China, Tonga, and Nigeria, already in service at the time of writing this book; January 2023.

These new digital currencies are created in the image and likeness of cryptocurrencies, but issued and backed by a Central Bank, with "stable, secure, and legal tender" value.

CBDC is the acronym for Central Bank Digital Currency.

The terms money and currency are different. Money is the physical unit and currency refers to the monetary unit of each country. For example, a currency exchange is a sale of, let's say, euros for the local currency of the country we're visiting. Operations that do not involve the physical movement of money, such as bank transfers or cheques, are called currency exchanges.

CBDCs are essentially currencies because they will be a digital version of the same money we use today, but instead of being managed by a payment service of a bank or card issuer, they will be managed directly by the central bank or by private companies contracted and duly authorized to manage the infrastructure necessary for their operation.

Therefore, considering their use, we could say that CBDCs are a means of payment.

As mentioned at the beginning of this chapter, CBDCs will be created in the image and likeness of cryptocurrencies, from an application on our phone, tablet or computer, commonly called a wallet, we can pay with our mobile devices, as we can already do today, by placing our smartphone to an NFC reader in the box of a trade, or through a QR code generated by the seller's terminal that scans our phone to accept payment from the screen of our phone.

Beyond the electronic nature and the analogy of using an application from our mobile phone with NFC or reading a QR code to authorize a payment, everything similar to cryptocurrencies ends here, because we must make it clear that, regarding the essential properties of a cryptocurrency like bitcoin, which are; decentralization, limited or finite issuance and permissionless system, CBDCs or Central Bank Digital Currencies are basically the opposite, the absolute antithesis of a cryptocurrency like bitcoin.

CBDCs will be centralized in the interest of the issuer, they will be subject to permission to use via a digital identity, and their issuance will be unlimited, just like physical money, so their value will tend to zero over time. We will discuss this claim below.

We will analyze these premises point-by-point by looking at the reasons given by central banks for implementing CBDCs.

1. Improve efficiency: a CBDC could provide a faster and safer way of carrying out transactions, which could increase the efficiency of the financial system by eliminating the intermediation of banks or issuers of means of payment.

2. Elimination of Fraud: Because cash is anonymous and CBDC currencies are not, a CBDC could reduce or eliminate the possibility of tax fraud or other crimes by eliminating the need for physical cash.

3. Controlling the economy: By having direct control over the money supply, central banks could use CBDC to control the economy.

4. Compete with cryptocurrencies: Governments and central banks may want to issue their own digital currency to compete with cryptocurrencies and maintain control over the currency in circulation.

Let's analyze the arguments one by one

1. Improve efficiency.

The current electronic payment systems that are so common today, such as cards, mobile devices and even smart watches, are so simple and convenient that the first question users will ask is How will CBDC benefit me over the electronic systems and cards I already use?

Let's remind ourselves that every time we pay with a card, which is a private means of payment and the most common in developed countries, we also pay the commission for using this means of payment. The bank and the card issuer charge these fees to the merchants, who of course pass them on to the customer in the final price.

Usually, the commission percentage is around 1 to 3% of the transaction value for credit cards and 0.5 to 1% for debit cards. In addition to this commission, there may be other fees charged to the merchant, such as transaction fees or monthly point-of-sale rental fees.

If we were to pay with CBDC in the near future, we could ask the seller for a discount for not using private means of payment. Since the seller would no longer have to pay these additional costs. However, it is very likely that governments, as a new hidden tax, or the central bank itself, to finance the CBDC infrastructure, will maintain these fees.

Finally, the cost of the infrastructure needed to operate CBDCs will not be low. These costs, even if they are hidden, would have to be covered in one way or another by public spending. The business of banks and payment institutions will be subject to public competition in this particular vector of the banking business, and this will have such important consequences that we will have to analyze them in detail later in chapter eight.

2. Absolute elimination of commercial tax fraud.

It is likely that governments and the central bank will force us to use CBDCs with a minor temporary incentive or, if necessary, with coercive measures such as the obligation to pay all fees, tariffs and taxes with digital currency, or directly by legal imposition.

Once in place, it would be enough to charge banks and stores an additional cost for using physical money, or to restrict the accessibility of coin and banknote exchanges.

This would cause merchants and businesses to refuse to accept physical money, which in practice would lead to the disappearance of cash from the streets.

Even without having to ban it, and at that point, virtually all transactions will be conducted through the CBDC, and the government and the central bank, as well as licensed private entities, will have complete and absolute information about all the money we spend and receive.

It will be completely impossible to avoid paying VAT and any other taxes and charges that may be added to the current ones.

Just think, when we give our children money to buy sweets or ice cream, or when we receive any income, VAT or capital gains tax and probably gift tax, as in Spain for example, could be automatically deducted in the case of our child allowance.

With the virtual disappearance of physical money in everyday life, everyone, including our youngest children, will inevitably need an electronic device or smart card to buy anything.

3. Improved accessibility.

According to data from the Federal Reserve Bank of the United States (FED), in 2019, 7.1% of US households did not have access to a traditional bank account.

However, this percentage varies significantly by education, income, and ethnic group.

For example, the percentage of households without access to a traditional bank account is 14.1% for low-income households.

By education level, 12.7% of households with a high school education or less do not have a bank account.

By ethnicity, 17.7% of Afro-descendants are unbanked.

The percentage of unbanked people without access to any financial services can vary significantly between developed and non-developed countries, reaching as high as 70% in the so-called "emerging markets". We are talking about billions of people worldwide.

The premise of providing these people with access to financial services with CBDC seems highly dubious.

We should consider that the first requirement to access digital money is an electronic personal identification. Identification that many of these emerging countries do not yet have, and of course an electronic device and the necessary infrastructure for those devices.

So probably all those people who do not meet the first requirement, digital identification, will be automatically excluded from the new monetary system.

A Universal Digital Personal Identity will be mandatory because it will be not only your CBDC wallet, but also your national ID card, passport, health card, driver's license, academic or professional degree certificate, public transportation pass, and even access to your workplace, home, and maybe even your gym.

Now consider the consequences of a government arbitrarily deciding to block any or all of these functions, including your CBDC wallet. Authoritarian governments could do this directly, but even democratic countries already have the legal tools to take whatever measures are necessary, including "temporary" asset seizures, for example, in the event of a "national security threat".

Think about what would happen in the event of software failure, natural disaster, war or force majeure, or simply hacking or identity theft.

4. The control of the economy.

Central banks have the disproportionate privilege of controlling the economy, or rather of trying to control it, because we all notice that almost without getting out of one crisis, the next one follows, and with each one the control, surveillance and restrictions on the economy and on individual and collective freedoms increase.

It is shocking to hear Christine Lagarde, the current president of the European Central Bank, advocate a CBDC because "it will be the only way to have the backing of a central bank", when any observer with a minimum of education in history or economics will realize that the management of the economy has been disastrous since the introduction of central banks, and especially since the beginning of the era of fiat money, backed only by the imposition of the binomial: Government + Central Bank.
Definition of Fiat Money: A currency that represents a value that it does not intrinsically have.

Fiat money has no intrinsic value and is not backed by the precious metal reserves of its issuer; its value exists because the law says it has that value.

Since 1971, when Richard Nixon "temporarily" suspended the convertibility of the dollar into gold as the world's reserve currency under the Bretton Woods Agreements (1944), money has basically been backed by legal tender, and the current era of fiat money began definitively, not temporarily.

The issuance of non-gold-backed money since 1971 has resulted in a loss in the purchasing value of money.

Between 1971 and 2021, the dollar has experienced an average annualized inflation rate of 3.87%, resulting in a cumulative "devaluation" of -85.05%.

Reference: US Official Data Org.
https://www.officialdata.org/us/inflation/2021?endYear=1971

The history of the dollar's decline and the chronology of gold.

To conclude this point, we must always remember this concept: **The more money is issued, the less value it has**.

To explain this, I will use a simple parable that you can tell your children so that they are not misled in the future about the causes of inflation.
Let's imagine that money has just been invented and the central bank has created 100 euros/dollar. If there are only 100 cans of tuna for sale on the market, and there are only 100 euros/dollar, nothing else for sale and nothing else to buy, it seems clear that the price of each can of tuna will be 1 euro/dollar.

(100 €or $ / 100 cans of tuna = 1 euro/dollar per can)

Now someone, not elected by the citizens, decides from his position in the central bank to carry out a QE (Quantitative Ease*) and creates out of nothing, by the power granted to him by law, 900 new euros/dollar.

We still have the same 100 cans of tuna, but the total money supply is now 1,000 euros/dollar. The reader will quickly guess that each can of tuna now costs 10 euros/dollar.

(1,000 €or $ / 100 cans of tuna = 10 euro/dollar per can).

The value of the can of tuna has not increased, it is still the same 100 cans of tuna, if each can now costs 10 euros/dollars, it is because the value of money has decreased and it takes more money to buy the same can of tuna.

Inflation is not the general rise in prices, it is the loss of purchasing power of money, and this effect is always a monetary event.

Remember this definition; the disinformation media will try to mislead you every day by making you believe that inflation is the result of "shortages" in supply chains, wars started by some dictator, climate change, or whatever absurd cause some journalist can come up with.

Inflation is always a monetary event, caused by the issuance of fiat money, not backed by an increase in the production of goods or services.

Now, when the central bank decides to create new money out of thin air, a process which the media euphemistically call "quantitative easing", or "QE", it does so by various methods which we will not go into in this chapter, but which will be explained later, for the moment in a very simple way and again using financial or disinformation slang, it initiates a "liquidity injection", it lends money at very low-interest rates to commercial banks so that they, in turn, buy public debt from governments and grant loans to companies and individuals, of course with a differential in these interest rates in their benefit.

Companies and individuals will pay a higher interest rate than the interest on the loans initially obtained from the central bank, and the difference between the interest paid to the central bank and the interest charged to governments, companies, and customers will provide the commercial banks with large profits from their financial intermediation.
In this indirect way, although there are several other ways, they manage to inject new money, which always creates an economic boom, and always with a certain time lag, when this new money enters into circulation in the real economy of companies and individuals, is when inflation finally appears "unexpectedly".

With CBDCs, creation and issuance will be direct and immediate, bypassing commercial banks, and knowing the track record of central banks and governments' addiction to spending more than they take in, what can we expect?
More money issued, which will steal value from ours, and more money spent, which will add to the national debt.

When citizens lacking the most basic notions of economics were informed on the television that the European Central Bank, or ECB, had created a "liquidity injection" of 2.5 trillion euros to save the economy during the pandemic, and that the ECB was "buying" 80 billion (new millions created out of thin air) of government bonds, mortgage-backed bank bonds, and large corporate bonds every month, almost no one was concerned about the excessive issuance of money.

Money created out of thin air, but which we will have to pay back with interest through our taxes and inflation, the so-called silent tax on the poor.

CBDCs will only speed up the process of creating new money and give central banks free rein to issue or withdraw money whenever they want, in a direct and immediate way.

5. Competing with cryptocurrencies.

One does not have to be very astute to realize that, observing the development and adoption of some cryptocurrencies, in particular bitcoin, the determination of governments and central banks to issue digital electronic currencies as legal tender seems to be a crude attempt to imitate, combat and slow down the adoption of some of these cryptocurrencies.

If cryptocurrencies, again specifically mentioning bitcoin, and the "tokens*" represented by cryptocurrencies called "stable coins"* with 1:1 parity, or at least intentional parity with fiat currencies, were to be massively accepted and adopted by businesses and individuals, central banks and governments would lose the "exorbitant privilege" of creating and controlling money, and thus controlling the economy.

A simple definition of a token*.

A token is like a casino chip, when we enter the casino, we go through the cashier and buy with real money the chips that represent money in the casino and are used at the gaming tables.

If we have any chips left when we leave the casino, we can go back to the cashier and exchange them for 'real' money.

The problem could arise if the casino's cashier is closed for some reason; then we would not be able to exchange the chips for real money, and those chips would have no value outside the casino.

CHAPTER 3.

Understanding Money.

History and Evolution of the Monetary System.

Money is one of those things that we rarely stop to think about what it is and where it comes from, even though we have all been using it since childhood.

We can find several definitions, but the most common is the following:
Money is any medium of exchange commonly accepted by society to buy and sell goods and services.
In addition to the first expected property of money, that it is generally accepted, it must have several other properties, the most important of which is that it stores value and is a unit of account for measuring or quantifying the value of goods and services.

The list of properties that we should expect a medium of exchange to have in order to call it money is as follows, in no particular order of importance.

1. Acceptance: Money must be generally accepted as a means of payment for the acquisition of goods and services.

2. Divisibility: Money must be easily divisible into smaller fractions to facilitate exchange.

3. Interchangeability: Goods and services can be bought with money and sold in exchange for money.

4. Unit of account: Banknotes and coins should have a numerical or standardized face value that serves to quantify the value of goods and services.

5. Reserve of value: Money should be a store of value overtime.

6. Scarcity: Money must be limited to maintain its value. **The more money is issued, the less value it has**.

7. Portability and Durability: Money must be easy to transport and store, and it must resist wear and tear.

8. Fungibility: This concept applied to money means that any unit or fraction of money is indistinguishable from any other unit or units of the same denomination. For example, the value of five $1 coins is identical to the value of one $5 bill.

So far, we have defined what money is and its properties, although there are several other definitions that we will see later, we will briefly review the history of money to discover how we achieved the physical money that we still use.

Undoubtedly the first form of transactions between individuals in a society was barter, our ancestors exchanged one good they had for another that they might need, let's take an example, imagine a Neanderthal who was very skilled at carving bone hooks with which to fish, but somewhat clumsy at carving arrowheads, if he wanted to eat meat instead of fish, he could exchange a hook for an arrowhead with a fellow arrowhead maker.

The problem is that the work, skill, and difficulty of finding the right stones to make arrowheads makes them more expensive than bone picks, so barter was so impractical that our Neanderthals probably quickly abandoned this system and most likely began to value their goods by trading them for other specific, easily quantifiable goods, such as beads, which they could easily wear, or shells, as long as there weren't a lot of shells around.

The reason for this is obvious: in a coastal location, the shells of marine animals may be so abundant and easy to find that they have no value as a medium of exchange.
With this example, we can see that beads or shells (if scarce at the site) have many of the properties of money mentioned above.

They were widely accepted by the Neanderthal group because they were easily quantifiable, fairly durable, and easily transported.
With the example of shells, we discover that when a good is very abundant and easy to obtain, it has low value, or rather we assign low value to it, this concept must be remembered every time we think about money, the value and the price of goods or services are very different things.

In the days following the terrible earthquake and tsunami that devastated Japan in 2011 and caused the Fukushima nuclear power plant disaster, an alert was issued for possible radioactive contamination of Tokyo's tap water. Until the alert was lifted, Tokyo residents could buy any luxury goods in the stores of Shibuya, but they could not buy bottled water, no matter how much money they paid, because the value of water could not be paid for with money during those hours.

This leads us to think about two concepts that are often related but very different: value and price.

A good can change its price quickly if the circumstances of its availability (also called supply) cause our estimate of its value to change.
If a necessary good is very scarce, it will be valued and expensive; on the contrary, if a good, even a vital one like drinking water, is abundant, it will have a low price.

Therefore, scarcity is an essential property of money.
After the radioactive contamination alarm passed and the supply of bottled water was restored, it quickly returned to its usual price.

With the progress of time and technology, our ancestors discovered that the best money, according to the properties mentioned, was metals, first bronze, and soon gold and silver. Their price was quickly fixed according to their characteristics; in the case of metals, the scarcest and most costly to find, gold, was the one that reached the highest value just because of its properties.
In the case of metals, the scarcest and most hard to find, gold, was the one that attained the highest value precisely because of its scarcity.
If we think about it rationally, gold is only valuable because of its scarcity, since its properties as a metal can be satisfied by other alternative metals that are more abundant and therefore cheaper.
Bronze and silver coins could be used to trade goods of small value, but gold was reserved for larger payments, although its weight and especially the possibility of theft made it risky to transport.

At that time, the goldsmiths, the first artisans to work with precious metals, invented the following system:
"Leave your gold coins in my secure vault, I will give you a paper note with my signature and seal in the form of a receipt or certificate of deposit, which today we would call a bill of exchange, and when you want them back you can bring the receipt or certificate of deposit and I will return your gold coins.

So, a paper note, signed and stamped by a goldsmith, was in effect the value of the coins stored in the goldsmith's secure vault.
This is the concept we call backing; the notes (today's banknotes) were backed by the value of the gold deposited.
Given the convenience and ease of transport of the goldsmith's certificates, depositors rarely reclaimed their coins, as they could cover their expenses by exchanging the paper certificates.

This was noticed by the goldsmiths (what today we would call bankers), who very soon began to create more paper certificates than the actual gold they held for their depositing customers.
This made them very rich, of course, and also allowed them to lend money in the form of bills or promissory notes and charge interest, even though they didn't really have enough real backing 1:1 with the physical gold stored in their vault.
If a depositor asked for his coins back, there was no problem because the goldsmiths always kept a fraction of gold for such cases.

The problem arose when, for some reason, many depositors came at the same time to collect their notes in the form of coins, only to discover that the goldsmith did not have all the coins because he had lent them to other customers.

The happy idea of issuing more promissory notes or paper money than they had gold is called fractional reserve, it is the essential core of today's banking business, and coldly analyzed it is actually a fraud, because the bankers make profits by lending money that is not theirs but that of their depositor customers.

However, not only is fractional reserve banking perfectly legal, it is also the most common way to create new money.

As I mentioned in the introduction, the reader may find some statements or concepts difficult to believe a priori because they remain hidden from the knowledge of the common citizen.

Approximately 95% to 97% of the money in circulation today is electronic and has been created by commercial banks as debt through the granting of credit.

Our current money is debt, it is created as debt, and at all times there is more debt than money.
Only the remaining 3% to 5% would be coins and notes issued by the respective central bank.

Reference: 97% Owned | Creation of Money | Finance Documentary | Debts Explained - YouTube
97% Owned (2012)
Director: Michael Oswald
Writers: Mike Horwath, Michael Oswald

How is this possible? You might think, well, let's explain.

Our money in a bank is nothing more than an electronic entry on an account that the bank keeps in a database in its computer system.

"It's basically an accounting trick.... Banks create money. They don't lend it out, when a bank makes what is called a loan, it basically pretends that the money is written down... it has to invent the liability... that's how the money supply is created."
Professor Richard Werner.
Professor in banking and finance at Linacre College, Oxford.

The borrower of the loan "receives" new money created out of nothing as a debt to be repaid with interest. Once repaid, this debt or liability disappears, leaving only the amount of interest paid as new money created by the bank.

But that's just the beginning, although we have mentioned the fractional reserve mechanism, let's take a closer look at it.

Fractional reserve is the system by which banks hold only a small fraction of their depositors' money on deposit, on the assumption that many of their depositors will not demand their money at the same time.

This allows the bank to lend its depositors' money to other customers in the form of credits or loans, but to keep only a small fraction of its depositors' capital in this reserve.

From the moment a bank makes a loan "using" the deposits of other customers, it doubles the amount of money in that loan, because the borrower can use that money with the promise to pay it back with interest, but the loaned money is still available to the depositors.

Therefore, this "fractional reserve" system creates a monetary aggregate that increases the monetary base, thereby expanding the amount of money circulating in the economy.

The reader may ask, what is the percentage of reserves that the European Central Bank requires banks to hold?

At the time of writing, it is **1%**.

Reference: Bank of Spain - Monetary policy - Monetary policy in the euro area and its instruments - ECB interest rates (bde.es)

For the United States, the reserve requirement for all depository institutions has been set by the Federal Reserve at 0% of eligible deposits beginning in March 2020. Prior to that, however, the reserve ratio has historically ranged from zero to 10% of bank deposits.

Reference: Reserve requirement - Wikipedia

What is the reserve requirement or reserve ratio?

The reserve ratio is a percentage set by the European Central Bank (ECB) that is applied to certain items on the balance sheet of credit institutions in order to determine the reserve requirement.

In the Eurosystem, the reserve requirement is set by the European Central Bank (ECB). Until January 2012, credit institutions in the euro area were required to hold at least 2% of certain liabilities, mainly customer deposits, with their national central banks. **Since then, this ratio has been reduced to 1%.**

In other words, for every €1,000 of customer deposits, banks keep €10 as a reserve and either lend €990 to other customers or invest it in the purchase of a profitable asset that the bank will hold.

Now we have in circulation: 1,000 + 990 = €1,990 from a deposit of only €1,000.

The borrower uses this money, buys something, and this money is deposited in the account of another person or company in another bank, or even in the same bank.

The second bank, or even in the same bank, with this "new" deposit of 990 euros, keeps 1% of this deposit, i.e. 9.9 euros (let's round off the decimals for simplicity's sake), and this allows it to lend the remaining 980 euros to a second customer.

Now we have 1,000 euros from the initial deposit + 990 from the second customer + 980 from the third customer, i.e. we have a total of 2,970 euros in circulation, backed by an initial deposit of only 1,000 euros.

Imagine that the process is repeated a few more times, again we will round the percentages for ease of compression: 1,000 + 990 + 980 + 970 + 960 + 950; in only 5 iterations of fractional reserve banking, we have about 5,850 euros in circulation, backed by only 1,000 real euros of the first deposit.

In this way, the commercial banks expand the monetary base, almost geometrically or exponentially, the more iterations there are, and there is no predetermined limit, the more growth of the monetary base is created.

But this is only the beginning, central banks have the magical power, or the exorbitant privilege, to create money out of nothing.

Central banks can issue banknotes that cost only a few cents to produce by earning the face value of the banknote minus the cost of issuing it, called "seigniorage".
Seigniorage from the Old French seigneuriage, "Right of the lord (seigneur) to mint money".
Is the difference between the value of money and the cost to produce and distribute it. In other words, it is the profit made by a government by issuing currency.

Reference: What is seigniorage? (europa.eu)

But there is more: although the commercial banks are the biggest money creators in quantitative terms, the main money issuer is the central bank, in the Euro system, the ECB or European Central Bank, which creates and puts into circulation as much new money as it sees fit in various other ways.

One of them is by "buying" corporate bonds*, from large corporations or from the banks with mortgage-backed bonds, with money that it does not have, but that it can invent "ad hoc", i.e. for this purpose, which we call the real money qualifier we use: fiat money, from the Latin "let it be done" already mentioned above: "money which represents a value which it does not have in itself and which is not backed by the precious metal reserves of its issuer, but only by legal imposition".

And even more: The ECB is buying up the public debt of some member states, especially those with chronic and structural deficits, such as Portugal, Spain, France, Italy and Greece, with money that it does not have and it is creating out of thin air for this purpose.

The reader should be aware that Article 123, paragraph 1 of the Treaty on European Union **expressly prohibits the subsidization or purchase of public debt by the ECB.**

Treaty on European Union. Article 123-1.

1. Overdraft facilities or any other type of credit facility with the European Central Bank or with the central banks of the *Member States (hereinafter referred to as 'national central banks') in favo*ur of Union institutions, bodies, offices or agencies, central governments, regional, local or other public authorities, other bodies governed by public law, or public undertakings of Member States shall be prohibited, as shall the purchase directly from them by the European Central Bank or national central banks of debt instruments.

Reference:
EUR-Lex - 12016E123 - EN - EUR-Lex (europa.eu)

In my opinion, the wording of the article is so transparent and clear that it cannot give rise to any other interpretation.
The German Constitutional Court felt the same way when, in August 2017, it referred a dispute to the Court of Justice of the European Union on the grounds that the financing and purchase of Greek public debt violated Article 123.1 of the Treaty on European Union.

However, as the popular saying goes: "As the law is made, so is the trap".

The Judgment of the Court of Justice (Grand Chamber) in Case C-493/17 (H. Weiss and others) considers that the Programme of government bond **purchases on secondary markets** implemented by the European System of Central

Banks since Decision 2015/774 of the European Central Bank of 4 March 2015 **does not infringe primary Union law**.

The Judgment of the Court of Justice (Grand Chamber) of December 11, 2018.
Reference: https://eur-lex.europa.eu/legal-content/en/TXT/?uri=CELEX:62017CJ0493

The purchase of public debt securities of member states does not violate the EU treaty if the ECB buys public debt securities in the secondary market.
So it is forbidden to do it directly, but it is allowed on the secondary market.

The reader may ask; What is the Secondary Market *?
What is the difference?

The first question can be answered in simple terms: it is a public auction of securities or bonds, in which the issuer of the asset does not participate, but other participants, such as investors and financial institutions, act as intermediaries, which, under the criteria of supply and demand, come to the auction and can acquire these public bonds issued by the States.

In simple terms, the ECB cannot buy the public debt of a Member State directly; it must do so on the secondary market from an intermediary, which will be the commercial banks, which in turn will resell the bonds they have just bought to the ECB at a certain profit and without any effort on their part.

This kind of intermediation and arbitrage between markets is what stockbrokers and bankers call "free money".

The answer to the second question: What is the difference? Virtually none. Since investors and other financial institutions rarely want to buy the public debt of southern countries, or do so in small amounts, most and usually all of the public debt issued by countries like Spain or Italy is purchased by the ECB "at auction" or on the secondary market, in this author's opinion, in violation of Article 123-1.

Despite the fact that the Court of Justice of the European Union has ruled that it does not violate Article 123.1 of the Treaty on European Union.

With this legal trap, the ECB is financing the structural deficit of the countries of the South, giving the politicians of these countries the wings to continue increasing the deficit until we reach the point where we will not even be able to pay the interest on this debt, since it has already reached a value that makes it unpayable.

Many economists describe the situation as "keep kicking the can down the road and we'll see in the future.

Another way the central banks create money is by lending to the commercial banks, the normal thing is that the central bank charges the banks a moderate interest, according to the interest rates they set, and the banks charge their customers a higher interest, making a profit on the difference.

Therefore, money is again created as debt; debt that must be repaid, but since there is always more debt than money, to pay the interest on this new money, more money must be created, which in turn creates more debt.

This is the ultimate reason why our monetary system is inherently unstable and unsustainable, and is considered by many to be a Ponzi scheme* or pyramid scheme.

And a Ponzi scheme has no solution until it collapses.

However, for the last ten years the ECB has been lending money at negative interest rates, which in the simplest explanation is an economic and logical aberration, since interest rates set by central banks are the price of money.
It is an aberration when a commercial bank borrows money from the central bank and the commercial bank has to pay back less than it borrowed, i.e. the Central Bank is paying for lending, or seen from another point of view, the commercial bank borrowing is charging the Central Bank for receiving credit. It is simply illogical.

In addition, the central bank charged commercial banks for keeping their deposits at the central bank itself instead of remunerating their deposits, in an attempt to force commercial banks to lend these funds to improve the economy, which never happened.

This anomalous and abnormal situation we have been suffering in Europe for the last few years, and because of the consequences it has generated, such as the runaway inflation crisis that Europe is experiencing in 2022 and 2023, during the writing of this book. Finally, the period of negative interest rates has ended with a sharp rise in interest rates set by the European Central Bank.

By raising interest rates, credit contracts, such as loans and mortgages, increase the interest that applicants must pay, causing a reduction or contraction in the number of loans, which in turn reduces the amount of money in circulation, which will certainly lead to a collapse in consumption, higher mortgage rates, and a certain recession.

By reducing the demand for goods and services due to the crisis, prices should fall.
However, there is a popular saying about inflation that goes: "Inflation is like toothpaste, it's easy to take out of the tube, but hard to put back in."

Let's review some important concepts.

Inflation is the loss of purchasing power of money caused by the issuance of new money.
The more money is issued the less value it has, so more money is needed to purchase the same goods or services.

Rising prices are a symptom of inflation, not its cause; the cause of inflation is always a monetary event.

Inflation is not a one-time event, it is a permanent, deliberate and inherent characteristic of fiat money, created and controlled by the issuer of the currency.

The money we know as the Euro, Dollar, Pound, etc. is fiat money that is not backed by precious metals, it simply has value by legal imposition in the respective geographical areas.

Money is created as debt; therefore, fiat money is debt.

Since all money issued is created as debt with interest to be repaid to the issuer, there is always and at all times more debt than money.

Forms of Money.

Money comes in many forms. But the most common are: cash in the form of coins and bills, checks, credit/debit cards, bank transfers and electronic wallets, promissory notes, and corporate or government bonds. They are all different forms of money.

Note to the reader that except for cash in the form of coins and bills, the above list mentions others that are not necessarily issued by the central bank, and all of them are a representation of money in the form of a record of a promise or obligation to pay, such as a check, bond, or certificate issued by the treasury or public administration of a state, or the key or physical object, such as a credit or debit card, that allows access or disposal of the money deposited in a bank account by means of a secret key, but in essence all of them are nothing more than physical or electronic written records.

As I mentioned earlier, most of the money in circulation was created by commercial banks in the form of loans and exists only as an electronic record in the banks' database.

Only in countries with a large unbanked population, such as India, is the amount of cash in circulation greater than the amount "deposited" in bank records, although the process of transition from physical cash to electronic money is developing rapidly.

India will move directly from a mostly physical money circulation to CBDCs thanks to the gigantic electronic and biometric identification program that the Indian government has implemented, as well as brutal coercive measures such as eliminating the highest denomination notes and those most used by the poor to store their savings by forcing them to open bank accounts.

On the evening of November 8, 2016, Indian television made a surprise announcement. In a live appearance, Prime Minister Narendra Modi declared that the two most valuable banknotes on the market (Rs. 1,000 and Rs. 500) would be withdrawn from circulation immediately. The demonetization plan, as the press called it, had been planned in secret and was immediately hailed as Modi's masterstroke against dark money.

The immediate result was chaos. People rushed to banks and ATMs to exchange their old notes and withdraw the new currency. Bank queues grew, many people suffered, especially the poor who did not have access to credit cards or mobile wallets, and dozens were reported dead in the crisis.

The Indian government's Aadhaar program was launched in 2009 to provide all Indian citizens with a unique identification number to facilitate access to government and financial services.

Aadhaar is an online identity verification system that uses iris, fingerprint, and facial recognition technology to verify a person's identity.

Indian citizens must register for an Aadhaar number and then use it to access a variety of services, including financial assistance, healthcare services, and access to social security programs.

In addition to providing access to government and financial services, Aadhaar has helped reduce corruption by reducing the need for physical documents and reducing duplication of financial assistance and other government programs.

Obviously, Aadhaar is the essential first step in the implementation of the e-Rupee CBDC.

Note the importance of this electronic identification in several areas that will allow the government to have full control over its citizens, without neglecting the practical benefits it brings in a country of 1.4 billion people.

In what we usually call developed countries, the use of cash is very low, almost non-existent, for example in the Nordic countries, where paying with physical money is becoming increasingly difficult as businesses and shops prefer the convenience of electronic means of payment.

We all associate money with coins or bills, but almost all existing money is an electronic record. It is truly amazing how a social abstraction we call money is considered real only because in its least used form, cash, we can still touch and count it.

I have on many occasions heard people very reluctant to consider the value of owning bitcoin, arguing that it is not tangible, it is electronic, "virtual" and therefore not real, although they are not yet aware that their money in the bank is exactly an electronic record, and even more virtual than bitcoin itself, since that record is maintained by the private computer system of a bank.

The island of Yap has a strange form of money. In Micronesia, in the Pacific Ocean, large stone discs were used as money. These discs, known as "Rai Stones", were hand carved from a special limestone rock found only on a small nearby island, not on Yap Island itself.

The Rai Stones were very large and heavy, some measuring over 3 meters in diameter and weighing over 4 tons.

Rai Stones were used as a medium of exchange for important economic transactions.

Once a Rai Stone was used in a transaction, its ownership was transferred to the new owner.

Everyone on the island knew about the transaction and therefore recognized the new ownership of a Rai Stone by associating it with its new owner. However, the physical disk remained in its original location.

This was because they were too large and heavy to be easily moved or stolen.

Rai Stones were considered valuable not only because of their size and weight, but also because of the history and reputation of their provenance.

Rai Stones are essentially a monetary record of a large transaction, but of public knowledge and acceptance by all inhabitants of the island.

We can think of the definition of money as a quantifiable record of the value that our work has contributed to society, or the value that farmers, fishermen, ranchers, manufacturing or service companies have contributed to society.

I particularly like this definition of money, just as I naturally rebel against money that is created out of nothing, as debt with interest to be repaid, issued by opaque institutions that are not even democratically elected, such as central banks.

Understanding money as a record still causes a certain amount of rejection in many people, because we almost unconsciously associate money with its physical form, and it makes them uncomfortable to think that it is just a record that can be easily lost, erased, or altered.

Let's look at a striking example to try to assimilate that perhaps the best definition of money is as a record.

After the invasion and armed conflict between Russia and Ukraine that began in February 2022, the United States, using its control over the Western financial and monetary system, first promoted the freezing or blocking of Russian state bank deposits throughout the Western world (where we must also include Japan) and immediately the bank deposits of all Russian companies as well as Russian citizens in an arbitrary manner, since many Russians will undoubtedly be against such a war.

Many Russian banks have been blocked and excluded from the banking interconnection system called SWIFT*, which in practice means an isolation of the entire Russian banking system, at least with Western banks.

The amount of money frozen, although it would be more correct to say confiscated, from Russia reaches about $300 billion in various banks and in various Western countries.

Without going into an evaluation of this act, nor mentioning the consequences, for which we would need another book, we can realize that in recent decades Russia has exported its valuable commodities in immense quantities to the whole world, not only oil and natural gas, but also grain, fertilizers, metals such as aluminum, palladium, gold, uranium, the list could be much longer, receiving in return those billions of dollars that were "deposited" as dollars and euros in Western banks, in quotation marks, because "deposited" really means recorded in some accounting notes, simple numbers in the computer system of a few banks.

The immense cost and labor involved in sourcing, refining, and delivering these large volumes of goods in exchange for digital transactions can now be fully appreciated.

When we realize that money is primarily a record, we understand how vulnerable it is and how easy it will be to block or confiscate your money from the CBDC application that will be forced upon us.

If you have bills or coins, you own them, and although they could be confiscated, it would not be that easy, you can always protect or hide your physical money.

When your money is accounted for as a number in a computer system managed by a bank, or in a CBDC system managed by the central bank and the government, it is no longer in your possession, and therefore you do not own it. You only have permission to use it, and that permission can be conditioned or revoked at any time.

Note that the same principle can be applied to a digital identity; if your identity information is electronic, it could be altered or deleted without you being able to do anything about it.

This argument has been used in novels and movies to describe dystopian worlds where the government could make any individual who proves rebellious disappear.

CHAPTER 4.

Differences from Cryptocurrencies like Bitcoin.

As I mentioned in the analysis of the "reasons" given by central banks and governments, CBDCs are the antithesis of a cryptocurrency like bitcoin.

Let's look deeper into the subject, we are already clear on several concepts, fiat currencies, like all current ones, are not backed by anything other than a legal imposition and the confidence we assume that the state authority will be able to exert whatever force is necessary to maintain that imposition.

Let's look at a quick list of the differences and then analyze them:

1 a/b. Issuer/Issue: A CBDC coin is issued by a central bank, while Bitcoin is decentralized and has no central issuer.

2. Regulation: A CBDC coin is regulated by the government, while Bitcoin is not regulated by laws, only by its internal protocol published in its white paper.

3. Privacy: CBDC transactions are monitored by the central bank and/or the government, while Bitcoin transactions are pseudonymous.

4. Processing: CBDC transactions may be faster than bitcoin transactions due to centralization.

5. Volatility: The volatility of CBDC coins may be lower than Bitcoin due to regulation.

6. Permissioned System: CBDC coins must identify the user or company and may have restrictions on their use, while Bitcoin is non-permissioned and can be used freely.

7. Adoption: CBDC adoption will be enforced by the government and central banks, while Bitcoin adoption is entirely voluntary and driven by the community of its users.

Let us analyze the differences.

1a. Issuer.
As we have seen above, fiat currencies are issued by central banks, although the money supply is mostly created by commercial banks through the creation of credit.
If the issuers, the central banks, are interdependent and not independent of governments, the criteria for issuing and setting the interest rates that define the price of credit and effectively control the money supply will clearly be set to satisfy the desires of governments and banks, and not according to social interests or the common good of society, to think otherwise would be naïve.

Bitcoin is issued according to a publicly known, pre-established and decentralized protocol that is de facto accepted by all its users.

No one, person, company or entity has the power to change the issuance criteria to their advantage. The criteria are predictable in the future and publicly known, and their use is voluntary and not mandatory.

1b. Issuance.

We must be very clear that the issuance of new money is a permanent fact, intrinsic to the fiat monetary model, where it is necessary to create more money to be able to pay the interest on the money previously issued.

Moreover, the temptation to create more money to pay for spending is absolutely unavoidable.

Virtually every government in the world desires the power to issue or control the issuance of money, which is the very core and heart of political corruption.

In fact, every government in the world constantly spends more than it takes in and disguises some of that money as being for social purposes in order to justify the creation of new money.

And the result is that the more money that is issued, the less value it has, because this new money dilutes or reduces the value of the previously issued money, creating inflation.

Milton Friedman:
"Inflation is always and everywhere a monetary phenomenon in the sense that it is and can be produced only by a faster increase in the quantity of money than in production."

If the issue of money has no limit, in mathematics we would say that it tends to infinity, then its value tends to zero.

This paradigm has repeated itself throughout history. All, absolutely all, fiat currencies that are not backed by a physically scarce asset or commodity such as gold have failed, and the current ones will be no exception.

When a fiat currency collapses due to loss of value from unlimited issuance, a terrible crisis is created, then the political power creates a "new" currency with a new look and lower face values to appear more valuable, forcing the exchange of the old currency for the new one with an associated loss on the exchange.

After the end of World War II, the new Deutsche Mark (DM) was created and reestablished by the authorities of Allied occupied Germany at an exchange rate of 1 DM to 10 old Reichsmarks.
This "generous" exchange rate was used to stabilize the German economy and eliminate the hyperinflation that had plagued the country during the war due to the Hitler government's constant spending to finance the war effort.

Unfortunately, the history of fiat money has always been associated with war. In ancient times, military expenditures were financed with gold coins, when the gold ran out, the war was over, but unlimited issuance of fiat money makes it possible to finance equally unlimited war expenditures, and wars are always used as a pretext to justify excessive issuance.

All this historical review shows us that the main difference between fiat money and bitcoin is that bitcoin, having a finite issue and limited to 21 million units as its first quality, establishes an absolute difference with fiat currencies.
The value of a currency could remain stable if it were issued at exactly the same rate of growth of the real economy, the growth of raw materials, processed goods and services, but quantifying economic activity is an almost impossible task given the chaotic nature of all the interactions that make up economic activity.

The issuance of new bitcoin units is halved approximately every four years, so we could apply the inverse rule to fiat money: if it tends to infinity, its value will tend to zero; on the contrary, if the issuance of new bitcoin tends to zero, a moment that will arrive approximately in the year 2,140, the value of bitcoin will grow and tend to infinity.

This mathematical paradigm can be so shocking that many skeptics refuse to accept it because we take it for granted that money loses value over time.

Some people call for a return to a monetary system anchored or backed by gold because it is a scarce commodity whose historical average ratio of new gold mined annually to existing gold is about 1.5% to 2%. This means, for example, that a Roman toga, reserved for freemen, patricians and nobles in ancient Rome, cost the equivalent of one ounce of gold, or about 31.1 grams of gold.
At the time of writing, an ounce of gold is trading at about $2,000 the price at which we could buy a good tailored suit today.

This argues that gold is holding its value and clearly shows the loss of value of fiat money.
Remember the previously mentioned fact that when Richard Nixon "temporarily" suspended the convertibility of the dollar into gold in 1971, the price was $35 per ounce and today it is close to $2,000.

This represents a 98% loss in value in little more than 50 years; following the trend we have described, the value of the dollar as a fiat currency, even though it is the most stable currency, tends to zero because there is no limit to its issuance.

Those responsible for the management of central banks are called central bank governors in most languages, in an attempt to give a halo of public authority to positions and entities that are not really accountable to either the government or the parliaments of the countries, in most of which the system for appointing their positions remains conveniently unclear or, in any case, little known.

The most important central bank in the world is the Federal Reserve of the United States, but it is actually a banking cartel* composed of 13 private banks called Regional Federal Reserve Banks.

The Federal Reserve System consists of twelve regional banks from different geographical districts of the United States and a central bank located in Washington D.C..

Each regional bank has its own board of directors, and the president of each regional bank is appointed by the Reserve Bank of its district and approved by the Board of Governors of the Federal Reserve System.
The governors of the Board and the Federal Reserve Chairman himself are appointed by the President and confirmed by the Senate.

So far, it seems to be a democratic institution, since its positions are appointed by the President of the United States and confirmed by the Senate; but as almost always, the devil is in the details, and the "little detail" is that the members and the governor of the central bank are pre-appointed by the FED itself.

Nominees for President and Vice President may be selected by the President of the United States from among the governors of the regional Federal Reserve Banks to serve four-year terms (Banking Act of 1935).
This nomination must then be confirmed by the Senate.

In other words, it is not the President or the Senate that appoints the members; they are nominated internally by the Fed and proposed to the President and the Senate for approval.

Since the Federal Reserve does not have shareholders like a traditional corporation, it is funded by the profits from its operations, not by shareholders.
However, the regional Federal Reserve Banks are owned by the banking institutions in their districts, and these banks are the shareholders of the regional banks.
However, the banks cannot control the decisions of the central Federal Reserve, and the economic benefits of the regional banks are retained by the Federal Reserve rather than distributed to shareholders.
The reader will probably agree with this writer that the whole structure that operates the U.S. monetary and banking system seems like gibberish that is difficult to understand, and I suspect that this is no accident.

By its name, the Federal Reserve could pass for a public body, but it is not, it is a cartel of private banks that have their shareholders, and the private property of these "Regional Reserves" belongs to the largest banking entities in the United States, although this is completely opaque to the citizens.

It is not a reserve, since it holds nothing tangible, which is the function of the U.S. Treasury, nor is it federal, since it is not a public entity.

Governors are nothing more than executives elected by the shareholders of the regional banks that make up the Federal Reserve System.

By definition, a private corporation engages in economic or commercial activity in pursuit of profit, or gains for its owners or shareholders, so it seems unrealistic to expect the Federal Reserve to make decisions with the public good in mind rather than its own interests.

2. Regulation.

Although governments repeat that regulations of all kinds are for our good and always to protect the citizen, the truth is that they are nothing more than the disguised use of government force against citizens to maintain control.

Economic and financial regulations are created to protect the interests of big business, especially the banking and financial sector.

Governments and lawmakers use the so-called revolving door to gain access to high-level, politically appointed political or civil service positions from which they legislate and regulate with the primary objective of benefiting the banking industry and controlling citizens.

Using public institutions that supposedly oversee banking, financial and competition activities.

When their time of public "service" is over, most of them use the revolving doors to return to the corporate world, occupying high and well-paid positions.

CBDCs will be the perfect instrument to control and impose the restrictions they wish to impose, always to "protect us" and in strict compliance with the laws; laws that will be created or modified as necessary for this purpose.

Bitcoin is a permissionless system, no permission is needed to create a wallet, send or receive Bitcoin.

Bitcoin transactions are irreversible, unlike credit card transactions and bank transfers, and cannot be censored, worldwide, regardless of governments, states or borders.

3. Privacy:

"The digital euro will never be programmable"
Fabio Panetta. Member of the Executive Board of the European Central Bank (January 2023).

Even if we give the benefit of the doubt to the words of the Executive Board of the European Central Bank, this does not mean that governments and not the central bank, under the usual pretexts of anti-money laundering and anti-terrorist financing, will exercise control or have full access to the information extracted from our CBDC digital wallet, also called the Digital Euro in Europe.

The most reasonable thing to do will be to assume that every single transaction, both sent and received, will be fully monitored by the government, a task that in practice will probably be performed by private companies subcontracted for this purpose.

4. Processing.

This could be one of the few clear advantages of a digital currency system, as long as it is properly implemented, transactions should be as fast and convenient as credit/debit card payments or mobile payment systems from major technology companies.

On the other hand, bitcoin payments to replace cash or credit cards would be extremely slow, since it takes at least 1 hour for a transaction to be considered secure and irreversible, which is the time required to confirm at least 6 blocks of the bitcoin blockchain, which are added every 10 minutes.
At this point, it is necessary to emphasize that not all payments require the immediacy of payment in a merchant, for example, billing between companies or direct debits of monthly receipts for services or rentals could be perfectly carried out with bitcoin.

In any case, although it is not the purpose of this book, the reader should know that there are already second-layer systems on the Bitcoin blockchain that allow instant micro-payments with Bitcoin through the Lightning Network system, which is already widely used even though it is still considered to be in the testing phase.
This system is being used in El Salvador to provide instant payment services using bitcoin as legal tender alongside the US dollar.

The Lightning Network system can be unbeatable in terms of capacity, speed and number of transactions processed per second, far exceeding the services most commonly used by credit/debit card issuers today.

By design, the more users that use the Lightning Network, the faster and more powerful it becomes.

5. Volatility.

Volatility is a statistical measure of how much the price of a currency or financial asset changes over a given period of time.

While we may think that a fiat currency issued by a central bank maintains a stable value over time, a cursory review of history shows that its value inexorably goes to zero, and inflation steadily erodes its purchasing power.
Unfortunately, during periods of high inflation, such as the current one, 2022, 2023, the accelerated loss of value is clearly observable, although the appearance of a fixed nominal value in banknotes and coins disguises this adverse event.

On the contrary, bitcoin, which still has a small capitalization compared to the fiat money supply and lacks a regulation that provides legal certainty to large institutional investors, suffers from an enormous volatility that makes it very inconvenient to use as a currency in the short and medium term.
Although it is in the long term where bitcoin shows an increase in its value, 1,800% counting only since 2014, with cycles of four 4 years, where one year is a big drop in price, for three years of increases.

Reference:
The Bitcoin Macro Disconnect.
https://www.newyorkfed.org/medialibrary/media/research/staff_reports/sr1052.pdf
Federal Reserve Bank of New York Staff Reports, no. 1052

Page #10:

"In about ten years, Bitcoin experienced rapid growth going from $5 in 2012 to above $60,000 in March 2021, for a compound annual growth rate of about 270% per year. The compound annual growth rate in the full sample is, however, 220% per year because of its recent decline. (2022) During the same sample period, the S&P 500 grew about 11% per year between 2012 and 2022, while gold and silver prices remained flat."

According to the above information from the New York Federal Reserve about Bitcoin price volatility and growth, we should consider the time period according to our expectations before making a judgment about it.

6. Permitted System.

Just like using the banking system, the basic requirement for using a CBDC digital currency is personal identification, the direct consequence of which is that users must have the permission of the issuer to access the e-wallet application in the first place.

Secondly, the registered funds and all transactions will be under constant monitoring, supervision and approval, which obviously undermines the real ownership of the funds, since at the discretion of the CBDC issuer, the permission to access the wallet application could be conditioned or revoked at any time, always under legal premises or for its "own security".

Likewise, any transaction that might violate the issuer's criteria or its government's regulations could be unauthorized, blocked, or worse, reversed.

Bitcoin, on the other hand, is a permissionless system; it does not require permission to install the wallet of your choice, nor to receive or send Bitcoins.

As a fully decentralized system, it does not require an intermediary or authorized central entity to verify and record transactions. Instead, this is done through a decentralized and globally distributed network of nodes that maintain a copy of the ledger, or blockchain, and verify and record transactions by consensus. This means that no one has central control over the network, and anyone can participate without permission.

Transactions are pseudonymous, not anonymous, we will come back to this point later, and cannot be censored, stopped, blocked or reversed as long as the user is operating their own custodial wallet and not a wallet or application of a custodian company or an exchange house, known simply as "Exchanges".

As Bitcoin insiders assure, if the user is not in control by holding his private keys from a self-custodial wallet application, and has his Bitcoin held by an intermediary, he will not really be the effective holder, and will be in the same case as having his fiat money in a bank, worse still, usually exchanges still operate today without a clear regulation, and are excluded from the financial system as being able to join a public or private deposit guarantee consortium, as bank accounts usually have.

7. Adoption.

The adoption of CBDC is imposed by the government and central banks, while the adoption of Bitcoin is entirely voluntary and driven by the user community.

Considering the advantages that a CBDC electronic currency would bring in terms of social and economic control, it would be unrealistic to think that the political power would desist from implementing CBDC because of the resistance of the citizens.

In any case, they will use the well-known Overton's Window* system, which could well look like this:
First, they will introduce it as a test, "guaranteeing" that it will not replace physical money, but will complement it. They will continue to make the current means of payment obsolete, soon the only way to receive any social aid will be in the form of digital money, they could continue to make it compulsory to pay all kinds of taxes in digital currency, at which point physical money will have practically disappeared from everyday life, and indeed, as is already happening today, if someone handles a relatively large amount in banknotes, he will immediately be suspected of handling illicit money.
This excuse would be enough to interrupt the "guarantee" of the non-elimination of physical money, since this would obviously be the favorite of criminals and tax evaders.

The question is not whether CBDC will be the only money in circulation, but when or how fast it will be implemented.
This process, like all social control processes using the Overton Window* methodology, will go completely unnoticed by the majority of the population; young people will not even remember what physical money is, or the need to carry some papers and a certain number of heavy coins to make small payments.

The use of bitcoin as a digital money that is not controlled by governments, banks, or corporations is completely voluntary. The natural human preference for choice and resistance to the imposition of CBDCs could lead to social reactions that remain to be seen as bitcoin adoption continues to grow.

We will explore this topic in depth in the final chapter, "Alternatives to CBDCs," where we will examine the success of CBDCs in pioneering countries.

Chapter 5.

Overview of the Underlying Technology and Blockchain.

Here we will analyze what a blockchain is: Blockchain, and why it is the preferred technology for managing bitcoin, money and digital assets, tokens or tokenized assets, and will almost certainly be the technical foundation for implementing CBDCs.

We will only briefly discuss what a database is, the definition of which could be as follows:
A database is an organized set of data stored and accessible in a computer system. This data can include text, images, numbers, and other types of information that are structured for easy access, use, and management.
Databases are managed by a specific type of software called a database manager, either directly or by other applications that can access and query the stored data, and are used to perform tasks such as searching, querying, updating, and analyzing data.

There are many types of databases, the simplest form would consist of a table or box with horizontal rows and vertical columns of boxes where we would write the information we need.
Let's take an example, in the first column we could enter the Personal Identification Number, and in the following boxes on the same line we could enter the personal data of a customer or user, such as name, address, phone, and so on.

From the identification number of the first column, we could query the rest of the data associated with the number of the first cell in the entire row.

Many of the most commonly used databases today are relational databases.

These databases have multiple tables in which they store different types of information, but all of the tables share a common index or reference column with the rest of the other tables in the same database, and with a specific programming language that allows information from any of the tables to be found, queried, extracted, and combined.

Common examples are MySQL, PostgreSQL, and Microsoft SQL Server.

There are many other types of databases:

Non-relational databases: These databases do not use a fixed schema and allow flexibility in data structure.

Object-oriented databases: These databases use an object model to store the data and allow relationships between objects

Network databases: These databases use a network model to represent data and the relationships between them.

Real-Time Databases: These databases provide high performance and scalability to handle large amounts of data in real time.

Each type or architecture of database has advantages and disadvantages.

However, since the birth of bitcoin, it has been proven that when security, reliability and immutability are required, blockchain database technology is the ideal technology.

When we talk about the transfer of value over the Internet, such as money or digital assets that will be transacted electronically over the network, we do not want to have the slightest doubt that it will be done with an absolutely secure system.
For this purpose, a solution based on a database architecture such as those mentioned above, and not on blockchain, could be used, and maybe some state will do it.
However, the risks associated with sending and receiving money digitally would be very high.

Let's think about some of these risks, for example, if the computer system that processes the transactions were to fail for any reason, all transactions would stop. The solution to this problem is to have redundant systems, where there are many processing centers, and although a large number of them could become inoperable, the remaining ones still in service could provide their function without causing a problem in the traffic of transactions.
If there is a single point of failure, such as a central processing system, and it goes down, disaster is inevitable. So, the solution is to decentralize to multiple processing nodes. Even if some go down, the rest will maintain service operations.

Another problem could arise if the database is corrupted by an error in the processed data, which could be due to human error, hardware error in data storage, or worse, a criminal act or hacking.

We could imagine a dystopian movie scenario where the entire public electronic money network was not only out of service, but the data, i.e. the funds in your wallet, had been erased or inflated, as well as the wallets of all citizens, the chaos would be total.

This could be reasonably solved by having backup systems, called backup in computer science, for both the database itself and the computer processing systems.
However, restoring data and systems from a backup may take some time, during which the CBDC system would not be operational.
The way to solve this problem is called in computer science distribution or real-time replication.
The database should not be stored in a single storage system, but in several, the more the better, the more secure, with the very important detail that all stored and used copies must be absolutely identical.

If a processing node detects data corruption, it could stop processing transactions, a service that would be covered by one of the other nodes, to quickly rebuild the integrity of the data from its local backup of the database, or from the database of another node that stores the correct database.

It is also a risk a possible access or even a modification of the accounting entries of the system by an external or internal malicious agent, which for example will create false funds in the system database, giving these funds to your wallet, at this point we must consider crucial security not only for access but for the modification of the database, and it is at this point where we can understand that the digital identity is absolutely essential to control this risk.

For all these assumptions, blockchain database technology has demonstrated absolute reliability, although it is not as fast or efficient as other types of databases, in fact it is quite slow, it provides the security, reliability and immutability required to process monetary transactions or value transmission, although it is less efficient in terms of speed.

This feature is not a defect of blockchain databases, it is a feature sought by their design, where absolute security is prioritized over any other criterion, using decentralization, distribution and immutability.

How a Blockchain Database works.

To explain how it works, I'll use the bitcoin blockchain as an example, because since it was created on January 3, 2009 at 18:15, the bitcoin blockchain has demonstrated absolute solidity, without a single interruption, working with absolute reliability, despite being attacked even with the means of government organizations.

However, I will abstract from the more technical details related to the Bitcoin protocol.

The author's interest is for the reader to understand the basic functioning of a blockchain database and the huge revolution it represents if we want to guarantee the security and immutability of the recorded data.

Many experts in information technology, economics, management, etc. already foresee a near future where all transactions, not only of digital money like CBDC or Bitcoin, but also of stocks, bonds, options, notes, contracts, real estate titles, ownership of all kinds of tokenized goods, digital identities, etc. - the list would be even longer - will be recorded in blockchain databases.

A crucial feature of a blockchain-based database is whether the access to query the data is public or whether this access is permissive.
On the bitcoin blockchain, access is completely free and all content is public.

With a purely digital monetary system based on the Blockchain, the transparency of public institutions and all government agencies could be audited down to the last cent, provided that access to the ledger contained in the Blockchain as a query is also public. There will be no credible excuse to prevent citizens from consulting or auditing public accounts and transactions on the blockchain.

Let's explain the bitcoin blockchain.
The bitcoin blockchain is a digital database that records all bitcoin transactions in cryptographically linked blocks, like an accounting ledger.
It is a decentralized and public system that does not rely on a central authority or main server.
The Bitcoin protocol establishes three types of actors in the Bitcoin network and blockchain, which are Wallets, Validator Nodes, and Mining Nodes.

The wallets have several functions, the main ones are to send and receive bitcoin, or rather the messages of sending and receiving Bitcoin from or to another wallet, which once registered in the Blockchain are considered irreversible and immutable, as well as to store the Private Key with which you will sign each transaction.
We must understand that a bitcoin wallet does not store bitcoins, it only stores the private cryptographic key that allows to sign spending transactions.

In fact, the more appropriate name should be keychain and not wallet.

Wallets connect to the bitcoin network and can display bitcoins received and sent, and calculate the balance between those received and those spent or sent. The bitcoin blockchain does not keep track of how much bitcoin an address holds, only the inflows (received) and outflows (sent) in the manner of a ledger.

When a bitcoin wallet is installed, a new private key is created using a cryptographic algorithm that can never be shared, and a public key or address, or set of addresses derived from that public address. Each of these is a long string of alphanumeric characters, which we call addresses, from which bitcoin or fractions can be sent or received.
The private key is used to generate the digital signatures of outgoing or spending transactions when we send bitcoin. The public key is used to verify the authenticity of the digital signatures generated with the private key without knowing the private key.

Cryptography makes it possible to verify mathematically that the digital signature of a transaction can only be signed by a unique private key, knowing only the public key derived from that unique private key.

The wallet application is designed to manage the entire set of addresses from which bitcoins or fractions of bitcoins are received and sent, showing the owner the outgoing or sending, incoming or receiving, and unspent balance.

When the user of a wallet decides to send bitcoin, automatically and transparently to the user, his wallet generates an outgoing or spending message, which very briefly includes his own address, the amount to be sent from the bitcoin or fractions of bitcoin he has previously received and not yet spent, the destination address, a date and time stamp, and the digital signatures that unequivocally prove that the bitcoin or fractions of bitcoin he is sending, called "Satoshis", have been received and not previously spent, which proves that he is the holder, until the sending transaction is completed and added to the blockchain, at which time the new owner of that bitcoin or its fractional Satoshis is registered, who will be the holder of the wallet with the destination address, and of course the digital signature that authorized this transaction is also included.

Each transaction contains all the signatures of all the previous owners of that bitcoin or fraction, so it is easily traceable back to the initial point where that bitcoin or fraction was mined (or minted) by a mining node.
This verification process seems tedious, but a computer can perform it in milliseconds.

In addition, the wallet will add a small commission to the transaction to compensate the mining nodes for processing this transaction, many wallets allow the user to select what amount they will add as commission, if we want this transaction to be processed quickly, as in the next block, we should increase the commission we will pay, if we put a very low commission, this could be delayed.

The volume of transactions at a given time determines the price of the processing fee. At a time of high demand for transactions, the miners will only include those transactions that have a higher commission added as a tip, since these commissions are received by the mining node that manages to close and include a new block in the chain.

The price of the commission for the miners to process the transaction is given on the one hand by the length in bytes of the transaction, which includes all the data and all the previous signatures of the bitcoin sent, and on the other hand by the demand to add new transactions to the blockchain.

Once the message or transaction is sent by the wallet to the bitcoin network, it is received by the validator nodes and the mining nodes.
At the core of the consensus protocol (proof of work)* are these two main participants in the network: miners and validator nodes.
A validator node is a team in the network that provides the first layer of checks to determine if a transaction is valid; they will verify on the blockchain that the bitcoin or fractions sent are indeed owned by the wallet sending the transaction, as well as the validity of the signature chain that is also included in the message, which allows the nodes to mathematically verify, thanks to cryptography, all the history of the previous owners of that bitcoin or fractions since it was created or mined.

Valid transactions are added to a memory pool called "MemPool", a queue of transactions that have already been validated but have not yet been assigned a block. Over a period of about 10 minutes, the miners take from this queue of transactions those that have a higher fee associated with their processing, as an auction, and add them to a block.

The miners compete to find an unknown hash*, called a nonce, which, when combined with the transaction data, gives them the right to close the block.
The winning miner, who finds the hash* that meets a difficulty requirement through raw computational power, closes his block and retrieves the previously selected transactions from the mempool queue and adds them along with the nonce hash to the blockchain.

Once closed, the block is sent to all nodes, both miners and validator nodes, which verify that the block was legitimately closed by the mining node that first found the nonce hash, and cryptographically verify the new hash of the block.
This verification is extremely simple, and it suffices to verify the hash of the last block added to ensure the integrity of all previous blocks with mathematical certainty.
Therefore, all nodes can verify that their local copy of the blockchain is identical to everyone else's.

Miners can also act as nodes because they have a complete copy of the entire blockchain. However, nodes cannot act as miners.

If a validator or miner node detects a fraudulent transaction, it will mark it as such and it will not be added to any block.
It could happen that a node, also fraudulent, accepts a false transaction, in this case the Bitcoin protocol establishes a majority consensus, so in order to add a block with a fraudulent transaction to the blockchain, it should be accepted by at least 51% of the nodes, since we are talking about 300,000 nodes spread all over the world, plus between 7,000 and 10,000 mining nodes, this possibility is completely excluded.

In addition, fraudulent blocks, or blocks generated by malicious nodes, are also marked so that the other nodes stop processing and accepting their blocks.

For your information, you can freely download and install a validator node with a fairly normal home computer, but with good storage capacity.

This is what creates the vast network of nodes that provide security for Bitcoin.

Explaining how to close and link the blocks that make up the bitcoin blockchain.

This part may be more technical, but is only necessary if you want to go deeper into the underlying technology, otherwise you can skip to page 71.

Bitcoin uses the SHA-256 algorithm, a one-way cryptographic fingerprint or "hash" algorithm created by the NSA (US National Security Agency) in 2001.

Basically, the algorithm generates a key, or fingerprint, as an alphanumeric block (consisting of letters and numbers) unique to 64 characters, from an input text; any change in the input text will generate a fingerprint of the same length but completely different, even changing or adding a space in the input text will generate a completely different fingerprint.

However, if you repeat the process with the same text, you will always get the same hash or fingerprint.

The hash of a previous block that has already been closed is included with the transactions that make up the next block.

Therefore, if any data in a block is changed, it will generate a different block hash, and from that moment on, all subsequent blocks created will have different hashes from the hash of the majority of nodes.

The mining and validation nodes, by simply verifying that the hash of the last block added is valid, can know with complete mathematical certainty that all previous blocks in the blockchain are original, validated and verified, guaranteeing the immutability of the data added.

This is the mechanism that guarantees the absolute integrity of the blocks added to the blockchain in each copy distributed among the nodes.

This point is crucial in a blockchain database, the absolute mathematical certainty that all nodes in the network store an identical copy.

The hash function of the algorithm is also used to generate the private key and public key used in bitcoin to encrypt or verify a message or transaction. This pair is also known as a private key and public key, or asymmetric cryptography.

We can verify with full mathematical certainty that a message, such as a transaction, was signed by the owner of a private key or private key, knowing only his or her transmitted public key.

Reference: SHA-256 Explained.
https://blog.passwork.pro/how-sha256-works/

Reference: SHA-256 Hash tool function
https://emn178.github.io/online-tools/sha256.html

Once the size limit of approximately 1 megabyte per block is reached, in which all received and validated transactions of the last 10 minutes are recorded, the mining nodes close the block, and to do so, in competition mode, they try to solve a mathematical puzzle that meets a difficulty requirement that requires extraordinary computing power.

The first Mining Node that finds a solution that meets the established difficulty closes the block, and this is where the magic happens, the digital signature or hash of all the contents of the block already closed and validated is included in the next block, in this way all the blocks are linked together, guaranteeing each one the integrity of all the previous ones, any modification of a closed block and previously added to the blockchain would generate a different hash in all the subsequent blocks, which would be easily identifiable by the Mining Nodes and Validators.

The difficulty of the proof of work, which allows a block to be closed and added to the blockchain, is to find a random hash called a "nonce" that, together with the text of the block containing the transactions of the last 10 minutes, must find a hash that starts with a given number of zeros.
If at any given time there are many miners with high computing power, they will find this hash in less than 10 minutes, so the Bitcoin protocol increases the difficulty by increasing the number of required zeros with which the block-closing hashes must start.

On the contrary, if the computing power or the number of miners decreases, we are talking about hundreds of thousands of specialized computers, and the blocks take more than 10 minutes to close, the protocol will dynamically decrease the difficulty, until an average speed of 1 new block per 10 minutes is achieved.

There are many different blockchains, including commercial versions from large manufacturers, but they cannot guarantee the same level of security as the bitcoin blockchain due to the simple fact that the bitcoin network has a gigantic number of nodes.

The expected characteristics of each blockchain can be very different depending on the utility sought; to assess the performance offered by a blockchain, we must look at whether it fulfills its function of storing information with absolute security, in a decentralized way, i.e. without a central validation authority, and in a distributed way, i.e. with an integrated copy of the data in multiple locations.

Many other cryptocurrencies and various IT solutions implemented with a blockchain do not necessarily achieve their objective; blockchain databases are appropriate if we want security, decentralization, distribution and immutability. The usefulness of this technology is given by these three factors, and its usefulness is focused on the reliable, secure and immutable registration of data.

With respect to the Bitcoin blockchain, we can say that even in the event of a massive Internet outage, a catastrophic event, or a reduction in the number of nodes, the response and integrity of Bitcoin is guaranteed.

The robustness and computing power of the Bitcoin network is currently the largest in the world, surpassing by several orders of magnitude any other dedicated computer network, including all the supercomputers of large technology companies, research labs or nations.

Here are some of the most appropriate applications for a blockchain database:

- Digital identities and security for access to cloud storage.
- Data registration and verification.
- Land registries, civil registries, commercial registries.
- Registry of smart contracts, transparency of public institutions.
- Supply chains, automated security, voting systems.

A great feature of the bitcoin blockchain, which is not permissioned and publicly accessible, is that anyone can access, view and analyze all transactions and the contents of all bitcoin addresses.

Remember that the addresses, which contain the inputs and outputs, are not associated with any name or personal identity, so we say that bitcoin is pseudonymous, not anonymous, and absolutely all bitcoins are traceable.

All transactions can be tracked using applications called blockchain browsers.

With an economic system based on CBDC, but built on a blockchain, it would not only be technically possible, but extremely easy to achieve absolute transparency of public accounts.

It would be enough for state and government agencies to publish their addresses on the blockchain used, so that any citizen could audit every penny of public money, as long as a publicly accessible blockchain, such as bitcoin, is used.

If the state arrogates to itself the power to control all transactions in our wallets, should we citizens demand a publicly accessible blockchain CBDC?

In the opinion of this author, the answer is utopian, but as we now know, perfectly possible and therefore achievable.

CHAPTER 6.

Use cases compared to current systems.

Digital Identity.

Card payments over the Internet have a potentially disastrous feature. When you use them over the Internet, you send all your card information, including the security key, with each transaction.

With bitcoin, the user sends a digital signature that guarantees that only the owner of the bitcoin sent could have generated that signature, providing only their public key and a hash or digital signature, making it totally impossible to find out the private key by knowing the public key, hence the name asymmetric cryptography.

With the private key, a different signature is generated for each transaction, because even if the sending and receiving addresses or the amount and chain of previous signatures of the bitcoin or fraction sent match, the time stamp will always be different.

The use of traditional credit and debit cards for Internet commerce has always been risky, using a technology that became popular in the 50's of the last century and was never intended for this use is still a bad idea and even with additional measures causes numerous frauds that, although sometimes assumed by banks or issuing companies, they undoubtedly include these costs in the price of their services, one way or another.

Reference

When Were Credit Cards Invented: The History of Credit Cards – Forbes Advisor

Credit cards originated in 1914 when the Western Union Company created a card that offered benefits to its most select customers. It allowed them to enjoy preferential treatment and a free line of credit.

In 1958, Bank of America introduced the first bank card, known as Bankamericard (now VISA). Also in 1958, American Express introduced its first credit card.

In 1967, the First American National Bank of Nashville created the MasterCharge card (now MasterCard).

Undoubtedly, the weak point of using credit cards for Internet use has been their security, first because the transaction sends its own security key, which is highly vulnerable to a malicious attack called "man in the middle".

This consists of intercepting the communication between 2 or more interlocutors. To do this, the attacker places himself between the two and intercepts the messages from A to B, knowing the information, while at the same time allowing the message to continue on its way.

The communication between A and B normally continues as if it were legitimate, but the attacker can decide whether to continue the intercepted message, whether to continue it with the same information or with other modified content, or whether to take note of the data and keys sent, which will allow him to impersonate the victim and make purchases with the impersonated identity, or worse, sell this information to other hackers, multiplying the danger.

The use of Bitcoin, a technology created precisely to be used on the Internet, solves this and all other problems associated with sending value over the Internet.

Users of their own wallets or exchanges* can be attacked, but the blockchain protocol and chain has never been hacked, since its creation in 2009 all attempts or analyses show the impossibility of doing so.

Bitcoin hacks can occur on the wallets or exchanges, not on the Bitcoin network.

A digital identity that allows its secure use, in the sense that it cannot be impersonated, and also respects the privacy and the right of individuals to control their personal information and prevent its misuse, is still an open challenge.

However, we can already see two different paths in development: the solutions of large corporations and governments, which always tend to centralize, with the consequent risk of creating a single point of failure, and therefore even "fairly" secure will still be vulnerable.

An example of advanced development is the one presented by the Spanish company Alastria (Alastria ID), funded by a huge multi-sector consortium with 600 partners, including large companies, SMEs, public administration and academic institutions, for the creation of a public infrastructure, but based on a permissioned blockchain designed in accordance with Spanish and European regulations.

The other alternative path is open source, decentralized, blockchain-based solutions that are not permissioned and have no corporate or government involvement.

Some of these projects are:

RIF Directory.
Directory is an identity layer supported by the RIF Name Service. This project is intended to work in the RSK ecosystem, Bitcoin's smart contract platform.

Sovrin.
This is an open-source project managed primarily by the Sovrin Foundation, a non-profit organization, and powered by the company Evernym.
Sovrin is a decentralized digital identity system. The platform is based on a hybrid blockchain using Hyperledger technology. As such, its use is public, but with restricted access through administrative permissions.

uPort.
uPort is a project that provides a decentralized digital identity system based on the Ethereum network. It is one of the oldest projects run by ConsenSys. It focuses on providing open-source tools and protocols to build the identity layer in this blockchain network.

The ideal solution, in which each individual protects the privacy of his or her own personal data and provides only what is strictly necessary to access a service, is still in its initial stages.

For now, it is advisable to be cautious about the information we share. In particular, personal addresses, telephone numbers or financial information. In this way, we will avoid being exposed to malicious agents that could cause us very serious damages.

Undoubtedly, cryptography and blockchain will play an important role in digital identity.
Many companies and startups have already implemented digital identification systems, but there is still a long way to go.

Towards a single European digital identity.

Reference:
European Digital Identity: easy online access to key services | News | European Parliament (europa.eu)

The European Digital Identity is advancing at a rapid pace in parallel with the development of the European CBDC, the Digital Euro.
As published by the European Parliament, Digital Identity is defined as follows:
What is the European Digital Identity?

The European Digital Identity (eID) allows the mutual recognition of electronic identification systems from different EU countries. In other words, it allows European citizens to identify themselves and verify their personal information online without having to rely on commercial providers.
What are the "benefits" of the European Digital Identity?

The European Digital Identity can be used to access public services such as:

- Requesting birth and medical certificates.
- Notifying a change of address.
- Opening a bank account.
- Filing a tax return.
- Apply for a place at university, either in your country of residence or in another EU country.
- Obtaining a medical prescription for use anywhere in Europe.
- Proof of age
- Rent a car with the digital driver's license
- Check into a hotel

This is just a sample of how Digital Identity will be needed for absolutely everything.

However, for all of the examples in the list above, the documents we already have would be sufficient, so no additional documents would be needed, except for access to our medication, which will of course allow access to our health data in addition to our medical history.

We must be aware that the entire infrastructure of digital identity verification will be outsourced to the giants of cloud services (Internet services), such as Amazon Web Services, Google Cloud, Microsoft Azure, which have already outsourced practically the entire public and even military digital infrastructure of some countries.

¿What would happen in the event of a crash of these services, a hacking or even a hostile action in the context of a hybrid or cyber war?

We should keep in mind that when our data is "stored" in a centralized computer storage system, it is no longer ours, but the property and under the control of the administrator of the computer system that stores it.

Understanding this concept is extremely important. It is identical to digital money.

When our data is stored in a computer system as a record of information, it is very vulnerable because the information can be easily altered or deleted, unlike a physical document in our custody.

The data you wish to associate with this European Digital Identity is highly sensitive and is currently specifically protected by privacy laws that should, in theory, ensure that it is used only with our knowledge and consent, and only when necessary.

If your personal information and medical records are stored in a computer system, this information may be accessed without our knowledge and consent.
This information may be altered or deleted, in whole or in part, without us being able to do anything about it.

Access, rectification or deletion of some of our data could be conditioned or restricted by the real owner of the data, the system administrator, under the orders of the government, not to mention the fact that being centralized, it will be vulnerable to hacker attacks.
We prefer to think that these things will not happen, but the truth is that they have happened in the past and will happen again.

Spain. November 11, 2022.
A hack through the Judiciary steals data of half a million taxpayers from the Treasury.
The Treasury has been hacked: a dangerous cyberattack steals the data of more than half a million Spaniards - Crast.net

The information services speak of an unprecedented data leak that includes the name, ID or address of some 50,000 members of the National Police Corps.

November 21, 2022.
Hackers hack into the Spanish Ministry of Economy
Spain's Ministry of Labor and Social Economy hit by cyberattack (bleepingcomputer.com)

Last Monday, a public employee saw them remotely accessing the network with all the economic information of Spain: the police are secretly investigating.
The cyber-attack on the CGPJ stole the data of all taxpayers.

These computer attacks were later denied by the government in a short communiqué without providing any additional information.
"All of the Ministry's cybersecurity systems are active and under constant monitoring. There is no such thing as zero risk, and extreme caution must be exercised in the face of Internet risks."
We would like to point out that a well-developed and implemented CBDC system could be very efficient for the settlement of all types of transactions in the financial markets, which will most likely be managed by means of tokenized assets registered in a blockchain.

As mentioned above, many IT experts predict that the blockchain revolution will forever change all the mechanisms of financial markets.

Stocks or securities, ETFs or shares, call or put options, bonds, trusts, loans, property titles, all, absolutely all financial assets will be represented in digital tokens and managed in one or more Blockchains. Each token will be associated with a digital identity, and all types of assets can be managed from an app on your computer or smartphone.

In this scenario, payments and receipts or monetary settlements of any transaction could be efficiently handled by a CBDC system.

It is very likely that two types of CBDC will be implemented: Wholesale, for the exclusive use of governments, banks, financial institutions and corporations, and Retail, for the private use of citizens.

CHAPTER 7.

Potential benefits in safety and economy.

As mentioned above, the bitcoin blockchain does not stand out for its efficiency or speed, because what it seeks is absolute security. The 10-minute period between blocks is necessary for a large number of nodes to validate each transaction. This is not a flaw, it is an inherent feature of its design, but it makes it of little use for managing fast transactions such as those required in commerce, unless the second-layer protocol Lighting Network is used.

In contrast, a blockchain with only a few nodes or a centralized database will serve a large number of transactions, as credit or debit card payment systems do today.
A centralized CBDC should be suitable for ultra-fast transactions, which could also be used to settle financial products that today rely on private interbank payment and settlement systems.
Which, once again, suggests that banks, at least as we know them today, will be completely useless and dispensable.

The mBridge project of the International Bank for Settlements will be the bridge that will make CBDCs globally interoperable, and with it, foreseeably, centralized global control.

A centralized, traceable and monitored digital money will make many of the common crimes very difficult; any theft will be virtually impossible, as the stolen funds will necessarily move from one wallet to another, all perfectly identified and geolocated.

Criminals will really have to find a new way to "liquidate" their illegal operations.

Full tracking by the authorities would allow detection of any fraudulent or corrupt activity, as long as the ledger of transactions could be publicly audited, technology will allow it, political power may not allow it.
Not only individuals, but also companies and public institutions would have a wallet and all their transactions would be traceable, it would be nice to think that in this way any diversion of funds could be effectively combated and those responsible could be identified.

The use of wallet applications on smartphones will be enough to eliminate or render unnecessary the infrastructures of current private card-based payment services.
Instead, these private infrastructures will become public, and therefore at public expense.

There is one major drawback to the widespread use of CBDC, and that is the need to be connected to the Internet. In the event of a natural disaster, power outage, or force majeure, wallet applications will need to be able to perform transactions, both offline and online, both payments and collections, using NFC technology or QR codes.
This should be possible at least for a limited time and for limited amounts.
Although it would be very difficult to provide completely offline CBDC solutions, at least occasional online synchronization should be a necessary feature to cover geographic areas without Internet access or with limited or no permanent access.

There is one point we can make in this section about possible advantages, although it could very well be a critical disadvantage.

That point is that if our money is a record in a CBDC application of the central bank, it would in principle be protected from bank failure.

The basis of the entire current financial system that we mentioned earlier, fractional reserve banking, in which banks keep only a small fraction of deposits in their vaults, is based on the premise that it is very unlikely that many depositing customers will want to withdraw their deposits or cash at the same time.

When this happens, and it has happened many, many times, the bank is unable to repay its depositors, then it must turn to the central bank, also called the lender of last recourse, which will provide the necessary liquidity, provided that the bank's assets, such as real estate, bonds, stocks, and loans made by the bank but not yet collected, can support the amount the bank needs to repay the deposits.

Usually there will be problems because the bank's assets may take a long time to liquidate or may not be sufficient, causing the bank to fail, a term synonymous with "bankruptcy".

During this process the bank will be closed or will have suspended withdrawals, causing serious problems to all its depositors, before the authorities execute the laws already established for such an eventuality, which would be in principle an Internal Recapitalization or Bail-in* and only afterwards the indemnities of the Deposit Guarantee Fund of your country will be settled, provided that this Fund has sufficient "funds" to compensate the depositors up to a maximum limit of 100,000 Euros per depositor.

In the United States this limit is 250,000 dollars, in Switzerland 100,000 Swiss francs and in the United Kingdom 75,000 pounds.

From the point of view of a European, it is easier to believe that a collapse of the Euro system behind CBDC or Digital Euro would be much less likely than that of any of the major European commercial banks, especially if you are a citizen of one of the southern countries.

But this could also become a fatal trap, because there would be no way to get your money out of the CBDC system.

With physical money gone, our money will only be an electronic record, and we have already seen how vulnerable and easy it is to block, seize or delete a record.

A crash of the Euro system (not an impossible eventuality) would have consequences best left unimagined as we will be trapped.

The concept that when you deposit your money in a bank or an accounting record in a CBDC system, that money is no longer yours must be very present.

From that moment on, you have a promise to pay, or in the case of an electronic currency, permission to dispose of your money. But permissions can easily be revoked and promises to pay broken.

The risk of fragmentation and collapse of the European Union, and not just of the CBDC system, but of the confidence and value of the Euro itself as a common currency, is a very real risk.

The value of a currency, as we have seen, can be legally imposed, but that value can disappear, because in the end the value is not in the law, but in the trust we place in that law to be enforced, by the use of coercion if necessary.

In Chapter 10 we will explore these and other risks, as well as possible remedies or alternatives.

CHAPTER 8.

Challenges and Concerns.

Disruption of the current role of banks.

Today we naturally assume that money comes from, or is created by, the state or a union of states, such as the European Union.
That the state has the power to issue money is such a natural assumption that hardly anyone asks why and since when.

The link between money and government is much more recent than one might think.
In the case of Spain, it was only in 1874, during the ephemeral First Spanish Republic, that the Decree-Law of March 19, promoted by the Minister of Finance, José de Echegaray*, put an end to the system of plurality of issue and granted the Bank of Spain the monopoly of issuing banknotes for mainland Spain and the islands, in exchange for an important loan to cover the financial needs of the government of the day.

Reference: Jose Echegaray - Wikipedia
Note that Jose Echegaray, an engineer and mathematician, was awarded the Nobel Prize for Literature in 1904.

This decree gave the other provincial banks the option of remaining commercial banks, without the privilege of issuing banknotes, or of being integrated into the Bank of Spain as branches. Most of the provincial banks were integrated, and only five chose to remain commercial banks.

Until then, the banks, which were always private, issued their own banknotes, which were nothing more than a receipt certifying the ownership of the gold deposited in each bank's vaults.
Money was private until 1874, when the Bank of Spain was granted by law the privilege of the monopoly of issuing banknotes.

It was at that time that the State granted itself the power to issue money, and when banknotes ceased to be convertible into gold, and the Bank of Spain was granted the exclusive right to issue non-convertible paper money, or paper money not backed by gold.

Reference: Bank of Spain.
Banco de España - About us - History - From the Banco de San Carlos to the Banco de España (bde.es)

In the United States, the central bank known as the Federal Reserve System was not created until 1913.
The creation of the Federal Reserve System was the third attempt to create a central bank. Its predecessors were the First Bank of the United States in 1791 and the Second Bank of the United States in 1816, neither of which survived. Nearly 100 years later, a new opportunity arose and 12 regional banks were created that now make up the U.S. monetary machine.

The history of the dollar, however, is tied to the United States' war for independence from the British Crown.
In 1783, after the victory in the war, the first U.S. currency was introduced under the name "Nova Constellatio" and the states were forbidden to mint their own money. This meant that only the federal government could do so.

On April 2, 1792, the dollar became the official currency of the United States by the Coinage Act of Congress by order of the government.
That same year, the Coinage Act was passed, providing for the establishment of a mint in Philadelphia, then the nation's capital.

This establishment was responsible for the circulation and production of coins. In addition, the American dollar was adapted to the Spanish "Piece of Eight", which was the world reference at the time, in its composition, silver, dimensions and weight, thus guaranteeing its interchangeability with it, and the decimal system was established.

References:
Real of Eight - Real de a ocho and Global Currency - (traveling-cook.com)

Colonial American Currency - World History Encyclopedia

The material to be used for all coins was also specified: copper for the half and one cent coins, silver for the ten cent, quarter, half and whole dollar coins, and gold for the five-, ten- and 2.5-dollar coins. This decimal system was very different from the rest of the foreign currencies with the purpose of establishing a new national identity.

The production of the first coins in the House of Philadelphia was not put into circulation until 1794, the coins which, as we have mentioned, followed the model of the Spanish "Piece of Eight", were of the same size and were also made of silver. They were in circulation until 1935 and were called "silver dollars".

The "Piece of Eight" was a silver coin with a value of eight Reals, minted by the Spanish monarchy since the 16th century.
It was the first universal currency and the first legal tender in the United States until 1857. Its design, size, and silver weight inspired the symbol of the dollar.

Introduction of the first green Dollar notes.

Abraham Lincoln Dollars were demand notes redeemable for gold or silver at seven designated banks in the country. These notes were issued in 1861 and 1862 during the American Civil War. There was also the Gold Dollar, a gold coin minted from 1849 to 1889.

In 1861, funds were needed to pay for the war against Southern secessionists, and Congress authorized the Treasury Department to issue interest-free demand notes called greenbacks, named for the ink used on the back.

Later, a new currency known as United States Notes or Legal Tender Notes, also green, was issued. In 1862, these notes began to have geometric patterns and fine lines that became a seal of the Treasury Department, details that prevented counterfeiting. This is the origin of the current dollar bill.
Note that, except for brief periods, the bills were promissory notes redeemable in gold.

The convertibility of the dollar into gold was "definitively suspended" in 1971, during the Nixon presidency, due to a massive flight of capital from the country and the crisis of the international monetary system after the Bretton Woods agreement (1944), where it was "agreed" that the international monetary standard would be governed by the

US dollar, but backed by gold, guaranteeing the interchangeability of dollars for gold, at a price of 35 dollars per troy ounce of gold.

This period of mistrust of the United States as a guarantor of the value of dollars, as if they were gold, began after Charles de Gaulle demanded the return of gold to France in exchange for the dollars in its reserve.
The war effort of the Vietnam War forced the U.S. government to issue money without gold backing, which increased mistrust, caused exchange rate misalignments, inflation, and volatility in the financial markets, leading Nixon to "temporarily suspend" the exchangeability of dollars for gold. Needless to say, the "temporary suspension" became de facto permanent and is still in effect today.

De Gaulle famously argued that a gold-based monetary standard would keep public spending under control and prevent an economic crisis at the hands of "the money masters".

Speech by Charles De Gaulle, 1965:

"The fact that many countries accept as a matter of principle that dollars are as good as gold means that Americans are indebted for free at the expense of other countries.
What the United States owes, it pays, at least in part, with money that only it can issue.
Given the serious consequences that could be unleashed in the event of a crisis, we believe that measures must be taken in time to avoid it.

We believe it is necessary for international trade to be based on an indisputable monetary standard and not on the stamp of a particular country. What standard? The truth is that "no *other standard than gold is conceivable!* "

Once money loses its backing or exchangeability guaranteed by gold, as a scarce commodity that prevents its uncontrolled issuance, and becomes a monopoly of state governments, a degradation of the value of money begins through inflation, which continues to this day.

The appetite for spending and the deficit of political power embodied in the states inevitably lead to an increase in spending without limit, or with a limit that rises as it is reached, and to its simplest solution, the issuance of new money.
From that moment on, government spending, military budgets and wars have a seemingly "unlimited" source of financing.

The assumption of the monopoly of money creation by the states is a relatively recent historical fact, since the value of money, which must necessarily be scarce to maintain its value, has been distorted ever since.

Every time central banks issue or create money out of thin air, as when they "buy" private bonds of large corporations, banks, and public debt of states, or when they extend credit to commercial banks, they create fake money.
Money as false as that printed by counterfeiters, because this new money is not backed by the value of new goods or increased services.

Even worse, the value of this new money drains the value of the economy and the money already in circulation, because it creates inflation, stealing value or purchasing power from your savings, the fruit of our labor and the real economic activity of businesses.

But the damage does not stop there, the false belief of political power that states can create money out of nothing, drives the appetite for unlimited spending by governments, and the misallocation of this resource extracted from the already existing money to finance the new political dogmas of each moment, as well as military expenditures.

The role assigned to commercial banks has evolved with the history of money, when money was backed by gold and deposited in the safe vaults of private banks, that money issued as promissory notes, apart from enriching the bankers, was at least the representation of a tangible non-inflationary value.
Kings and states used to need the credit provided by the banks, until finally the political power took over the monopoly of money issue, from that moment on the commercial banks became an interdependent appendix of the political power.

Commercial banks obtain their profits, among other things, from the difference between the interest they pay when borrowing money from the central bank and the interest they charge their customers, individuals, companies and states, at which point the idea or question arises: Why should governments finance their public deficits by borrowing from commercial banks when they could obtain this cheaper financing directly from the issuer of fiat money, the central bank?

Another way in which commercial banks benefit is through bank intermediation in the processing of money transfers and custodial services, but with CBDCs, transactions will be made directly between wallets without the need for bank intermediation, and the custodial service will be completely unnecessary as the money issuer and the digital wallet applications or wallets will have to guarantee this custody.

Mortgage and consumer lending by banks could quickly be threatened by the government itself or by the issuer of the CBDC, since the privilege of having access to the full economic information of customers and businesses, and thus to the credit risk of the applicant customers, would give banks an insurmountable advantage in unfair competition with governments or central banks.

If CBDCs are successfully implemented, commercial banks may become completely unnecessary; the very existence of these banks, at least in the form we know them today, will be doubtful unless the political power finds a way to give them some of the benefits of intermediation.
Undoubtedly, during the process of implementing CBDCs, banks will play a role that is still necessary, but foreseeably unnecessary in the near future, once CBDCs are in place.

It is likely that the power behind today's banking institutions will not be a reliable long-term ally of political power in the process of implementing CBDCs.
Also, banks are often seen as enemies of bitcoin as a possible future money, but this does not have to be the case. Banks make their business by providing credit and financial services to their customers, this model can and probably will be replaced by CBDC payment systems, but if bitcoin continues to gain acceptance, this could be a type of money that does not necessarily have to kill the banking business model.

Many people will not want to take on the responsibility of self-custodianship or learn how to trade bitcoin; banks could provide credit and services to buy, sell, and store bitcoin as a back-up for savings that citizens refuse to hold in CBDCs, and protect them from the currency debasement accelerated by the introduction of CBDCs and the arbitrary decisions of their government.

According to the Bank of England's public document published in February 2023:
The digital pound: A new form of money for households and businesses?
Reference:
https://www.bankofengland.co.uk/paper/2023/the-digital-pound-consultation-paper
Contains licensed public domain information.
Open Government License v3.0

"The Digital Pound will be a public-private partnership or collaboration. Private sector companies, which could be banks or licensed non-bank companies, could be integrated into the core infrastructure of the Digital Pound and provide the interface between the bank and the users.

They would do this by offering digital "portal" wallets to end users. The wallets could be integrated with their other services. They are called "transfer" wallets (hereafter simply "wallets") because the user's digital pound holdings are recorded anonymously in the bank's central ledger to "protect your privacy," and the wallet simply passes instructions from the user to the central ledger. End users would interact with these wallets rather than directly with the bank.

Users would dispose of digital pounds by using their wallet to view their balance and to instruct payments and transfers of digital pounds. It is likely that most people would access the wallet through their smartphone, but there would be alternative options, such as a smart card. "

As can be seen, the private sector and the necessary infrastructure for the Digital Pound platform will be provided at least in part by commercial banks and "approved" financial companies, as well as the wallet applications themselves and their maintenance.

It cannot be ignored that all this will come at a cost, if we think that the digital pound, even with quantity limits, will reduce the capitalization of bank funds, as well as create competition in the payment systems business, CBDCs will not be well regarded by banks, unless they make some profit. One way or another, this cost will be borne by citizens.

According to Bank of Spain, gross fees for payment services represent approximately **one third** of Spanish banks' fee income in their Spanish business.
Payment services account for 4,472 million euros in revenues for Spanish banks. 31.2% of the total)
Referencia: Bank of Spain.
Financial Stability Report. Spring 2022. (bde.es)

How will banks be able to handle the threat or competition from public electronic payments through CBDC?
Undoubtedly, a massive implementation of CBDC will have to establish a new role of financial institutions with the political power that we will have to pay attention to in the future.

In the same Bank of England document, without explicitly mentioning it, it is suggested that "to safeguard financial stability", at least initially, limits will be set on the amount of digital pounds that a user can store in his or her wallet.

This is obviously intended to prevent savers from withdrawing their funds from banks to deposit them in digital pounds, which would create a very serious problem for banks.

However, page #17 of the document adds:

"Unlike cash, the amount of digital pounds that an individual or firm could hold would be subject to some limits, at least for an introductory period. This would ensure a smooth introduction without unintended consequences for monetary or financial stability.

These restrictions would still allow individuals to use the digital pound for their daily transactions, including receiving their payments. It would be for a new decision, in the light of experience, as to whether **such restrictions should be made permanent.**"

More references: Coindesk.com (Feb-07-2023)
Digital Pound Holdings Could Be Limited to 10K, Central Bank Says (coindesk.com)
The Bank of England has set out technical features of its central bank digital currency, which officials have said is likely to be needed.

On page #16 it states:

"The digital pound would be designed to support the Government's and the Bank's commitments to mitigating climate change."

In other words, it anticipates that there will be restrictions, though of course for "well-justified" reasons.

The general characteristics of the digital pound announced in the Bank of England document would be as follows:

1. It will be a consortium or public-private partnership project.
2. The digital pound will be used by households and businesses.
3. The issuance of digital money and the platform will be operated by the central bank.
4. The digital pound will be perfectly interchangeable with other forms of money such as cash or bank deposits.
5. Wallet applications will be provided by the private sector.
6. It will be used through smart phones and cards.
7. It will have privacy protection like bank accounts and cards, but it will NOT be anonymous.
8. No interest will be paid.
9. The Bank of England and the Government will not see any personal information.
10. The amount of the deposit would be limited, at least initially.
11. It would be available to UK and non-UK residents.
12. It will be usable for everyday physical and online shopping.

Even with a superficial analysis of the features announced by the Bank of England, we can find some highly suspicious contradictions.

Let's look at the contradictions or inconsistencies:

Number 1: The issuance and the platform will be operated by the Bank of England, but it will be a consortium or public-private partnership (?), furthermore the wallets will be offered by the private sector (?).

Number 2: It will have the same privacy as the bank cards and bank accounts, (which is equal to zero privacy); but it will NOT be anonymous, also the Bank of England and the government will not see any personal data (?).

CHAPTER 9.

Likely Evolution and Implications for Geopolitics and the Global Economy.

On page #16 of the same Bank of England paper on the Digital Pound, it is written:

"Although a digital pound would be designed with UK users in mind, it would also be available to non-UK residents."

This detail is very important when considering how digital currencies or CBDCs will affect the global economy and geopolitics once they are widely adopted, because as mentioned at the beginning of the book, almost every central bank and government in the world is working on developing a digital currency.

Currently, although the treaty of the European Union guarantees the free movement of people, goods, services, and capital across the Union, European citizens face many administrative barriers to opening a bank account in another EU country.

The use of a bank account abroad, even within the European Union and for an EU citizen, is only possible through private banking services, which generally require a capital of between three hundred thousand and one million euros.

However, it is relatively easy to open an account with one of the new "neo-banks". Neo-banks are financial institutions that operate exclusively online, without physical offices, and offer limited services such as current accounts, cards, money transfers and cryptocurrencies, but do not offer services typical of large traditional banks such as investment portfolios, consumer loans and even less mortgage loans, i.e. they do not really compete with the bulk of traditional banking. These banks also tend to have limits or restrictions on operating with high amounts, which may be very convenient for their users, but in reality, try to restrict the free movement of capital.

Initially, when these banks became popular, they offered bank account numbers (called IBANs in the EU) of their countries of origin, such as the United Kingdom, Germany, some in the Baltic republics, etc., but the major service providers in each country began to create problems with direct debit of bills for services such as telephone, water, energy, etc. to foreign IBAN accounts, even if they had European IBANs. This again violated the principles of free movement of capital and services within the EU, but forced these banks to set up "legal" branches in each country, offering their own IBAN for each EU country.

This change had several objectives, first of all to improve the usefulness of their services to customers in each country, but in fact, it hides that, for example, Spanish IBAN accounts, although provided by a German bank, are actually controlled by the Central Bank of Spain, i.e. it is actually to maintain national control of money, ensuring that they do not compete with the bulk of banking business, such as the credit market with large traditional banks in each country.

This type of operation actually hides a tacit agreement between banks, or what we could rather call a banking cartel, i.e. an agreement between companies to avoid mutual competition, in this case with banking services.

Of course, agreements between companies to avoid competition are also illegal and violate another EU principle, such as the principle of free competition.

However, CBDCs could radically and forever change the relationships between customers, banks, countries and currencies in a disruptive way that we can only guess at by doing an exercise of imagination about the new possibilities and inconveniences they could create.

From the moment a currency is issued in electronic form, borders cease to exist, and its use will be "standard" throughout the world.
While the international banking cartel is reluctant to allow free competition in their sector, CBDC e-currency issuers will clearly be in favor of allowing foreign citizens to buy and use their new digital currency, which would result in a juicy incoming flow of foreign currency into the funds of any CBDC-issuing central bank.

Ever since China launched the Digital Yuan, which is currently in use or in very advanced testing, there has been speculation that it would be used as an "economic weapon" to gain global monetary supremacy to displace the dollar in international trade, which has done nothing but accelerate the process of creating and developing digital currencies by all the world's central banks with the clear intention of promoting the international use of their digital currency.

The control and issuing power of the world's reserve currency gives the nation that issues it an exorbitant privilege, as well as some minor inconveniences.

The greatest power of the United States is not its enormous army, but its enormous power to control the economy and international trade through the dollar.

Without going into depth on this subject, which would be enough for another book, all issuers of CBDC digital currencies will be interested in having their digital currency bought and used by as many users as want it and can pay for its acquisition.

Let's consider likely scenarios.

The transformation of the Chinese yuan into an international currency is "a necessary condition for maintaining peace in the world".

So says Ju Jiandong, head professor of the School of Finance at Tsinghua University (Beijing), in an article published on February 28th in the Chinese state newspaper Reference: Global Times.

Professor Ju Jiandong, points out that: The U.S. may unleash wars to "protect the dollar" given China's economic growth.

As we can see, the "currency war" is not so likely, it is already announced.

China will eventually open its digital yuan to all citizens of the world, it is easy to imagine that citizens of all emerging countries, who are forced to use their national currencies and suffer from a permanent confiscation of wealth throughout history in inflation mode, immediately prefer to start buying, selling and saving in digital yuan.

Let's think about geographical scenarios with underdeveloped countries in Africa, Asia or Latin America, if you were a citizen of Liberia, Ghana, Ecuador, Nicaragua, Argentina, Turkey, Lebanon ...... The list would be enormous.

Which currency would you prefer to use, your local currency that is stealing its value with inflation from the moment you receive it, or would you prefer to save in a stronger currency that will retain its value?

At the time of writing this book, the beginning of 2023, the annual inflation suffered by Argentines is already around 100%, this situation is worse in some countries, better in others, is the normality, if we exclude the developed countries that have convertible currencies such as the US dollar, the Euro, the British pound, the Japanese yen, the Chinese yuan, etc., the local currencies become a machine of permanent confiscation of wealth.
In fact, this confiscation also occurs in the developed countries, only the process is slower, except in times like the present, when the inflation data, conveniently "cooked up" by the governments, has reached double digits in Europe.

How can an Argentine worker save a certain amount of money for retirement or simply for unforeseen expenses?

As soon as the United States begins to issue its Digital Dollars to foreign citizens, and it will no doubt be strongly encouraged to do so in order to limit the issuance of the Digital Yuan around the world, every Argentine worker will immediately convert his monthly salary in Argentine Pesos into Digital Dollars, thus preserving somewhat better the value of his work.

The Argentine worker will soon discover that the bakery, supermarket, and gas station in his neighborhood are doing the same thing, and he will agree to pay for his bread, groceries, or gas directly in Digital Dollars without having to exchange them back into Argentine Pesos.

With this example, still imaginary but highly probable, we can foresee a scenario in which strong CBDC currencies could literally cause a "mass extinction" of weak national currencies.

Will the Argentine government be able to prevent its citizens from using the digital dollar to the detriment of the Argentine peso?
Massive use of the digital dollar will lead to the irrelevance of the Argentine peso.
What political changes can we expect from the disruption of CBDC digital currencies in all countries with weak currencies?
There will undoubtedly be a global currency war, a war that has always existed but that physical money, borders and banking have slowed down or rather hidden.

There have always been tax havens and countries that have used their developed financial industry to provide offshore financial services*, both legal and non-legal, to wealthy clients, the best example of this practice is undoubtedly the UK, with its multitude of offshore jurisdictions, but also countries such as Switzerland, the Netherlands, Ireland, Luxembourg, etc.

Some of these countries, let's take Switzerland as an example, might be very interested in offering financial services and legal security to foreign users of their digital currency.

Switzerland would be very interested in offering its digital Swiss franc to anyone who can buy it.

106

If a citizen of Spain, Italy or Greece sees the value of the Euro falling rapidly, or distrusts the solvency of his country or government, he will probably want to keep some of his savings in Digital Swiss Francs.

Of course, there is also the possibility that local businesses in Spain or Italy will start accepting Digital Swiss Francs instead of Euros.
Will local political power be able to stop the use of foreign digital currencies?

We can extrapolate this possible digital currency war to the whole world, it is not hard to imagine a currency war in Africa where the Chinese Yuan becomes the dominant currency, or on the Latin American front a war between the Digital Dollar and the Digital Yuan.

Another effect that has yet to be measured is the impact that the use of digital money will have on payment service providers, all of which are of American origin and in use in the West, and which will be practically unnecessary unless they adapt to the new circumstances by offering new services.

It is very likely that there will be exchange services between digital currencies CBDC or between Bitcoin and CBDC.
I am sure that just as today there are already multi-currency and multi-cryptocurrency wallets, cards, and applications from fintech companies*, these will allow us to keep our money in different CBDCs or cryptocurrencies, automatically exchanging between them at our convenience, or recharging prepaid smart cards from any of these CBDCs or cryptocurrencies.

While there is a fee associated with each of these exchanges, consider that an Argentine citizen will gladly pay a 3% fee to avoid a 50% loss in value of the Argentine Peso, with an annual inflation rate of 100%.

There are a variety of circumstances that could turn out to be terrible with the introduction of CBDC currencies.
Let's imagine that the United States restricts the use of digital dollars to U.S. citizens only, and stops issuing or removes physical money from circulation.
Millions of people, especially in emerging markets and Latin America, hold their savings and use dollar bills on a daily basis; all of them could find from one day to the next that their bills are no longer accepted, or simply that the issuer of digital dollars will not allow them to purchase the new CBDC dollars if they do not have US citizenship or a bank account denominated in dollars, which is quite likely to be the case.

If all the dollars in circulation around the world were returned to the United States, it would cause hyperinflation that could ruin its economy; the transition to digital could be used to eliminate this risk, with terrible consequences for holders of physical dollars in emerging markets.
From a geopolitical point of view, the potential destruction of weak national currencies could, in turn, bring about the downfall of the governments of many countries that are supported only by the imposition of a local currency.
Of course, zones of monetary influence will be created according to the CBDC prevailing in each region of the world.
However, there is already a mechanism by which poor or underdeveloped countries could have a CBDC currency.
The mBridge* project is a Chinese-led initiative to create an international payment platform based on central bank digital currencies (CBDCs).

The project involves the central banks of China, Hong Kong, Thailand and the United Arab Emirates, as well as the BIS* or Bank for International Settlements.

The aim of the project is to facilitate cross-border transactions between the participating economies and to improve the efficiency and security of payment systems. The mBridge project is seen as an important step towards the internationalization of the digital yuan and a possible alternative to the US dollar as the world's reserve currency.

This project would allow countries with little infrastructure to issue a "customized" CBDC that would function in this way:
A poorly developed country, but with certain natural resources, or with foreign exchange or gold reserves, could go to the BIS* and, by contributing those foreign currency reserves, gold, or by pledging its natural resources, could obtain the issuance of a customized CBDC for the value of the reserves contributed, with a pre-determined exchange rate.

References:

Bank for International Settlement.

Multi-CBDC arrangements and the future of cross-border payments.
https://www.bis.org/publ/bppdf/bispap115.htm

Project mBridge: Connecting economies through CBDC.
https://www.bis.org/about/bisih/topics/cbdc/mcbdc_bridge.htm

The Bank for International Settlements (BIS) is an international financial institution, headquartered in Basel, Switzerland, owned by the central banks of various countries, which promotes international monetary and financial cooperation and serves as the central bank for national central banks.

The BIS also develops public technology solutions to support central banks and improve the functioning of the financial system through its Technology Innovation Hub.

The BIS promulgates or enforces a de facto set of standards that apply to the entire global banking system.

CHAPTER 10.

Application in Real Life.

Control, Surveillance and Restriction of Freedom.

The use of Central Bank Digital Currencies (CBDCs) as a surveillance tool, combined with other control tools such as social networks, cell phones with default geolocation, facial recognition, and license plate recognition in cars, pose a threat that many citizens would prefer to ignore and believe will not be implemented. However, they herald a dystopian and Orwellian world even worse than the one described in his famous novel "1984"

This process, promoted by the media of disinformation, can be carried out in steps, gradually, as described in the political theory of the Overton Window.

The Overton Window is a political theory that describes how social opinion can change in several stages (or a window of time) so that an idea that is initially completely unacceptable can eventually and gradually be introduced and accepted by society.

As an example, although in ancient times there were safe conducts to move through different kingdoms or countries, it was not until after World War II that the requirement to have a " permission" or passport to travel was introduced.

In the late 19th century and until World War I, passports were generally not required for travel within Europe, and crossing borders was easy. Few people had passports, and they were very simple, containing only a description of the passport holder. As the use of photography became widespread in the early decades of the 20th century, photographs were added to passports.

During World War I, European governments introduced this type of document for security reasons and to control the emigration of citizens with education or skills useful to the war effort, thus keeping potential workers within their borders. These controls were maintained after the war and became standard procedure.

In 1920, the predecessor of the UN, the League of Nations, held a conference on passports and tickets, which resulted in guidelines that were further developed at conferences in 1926 and 1927. Finally, in 1980, passports were standardized under the auspices of the International Civil Aviation Organization (ICAO).

Today, no one questions why citizens must ask the government to issue a passport, which is essentially a license to travel; it is so much taken for granted that we do not even think about the reason for this administrative permission.

Absolute surveillance is only the first step, with the information obtained in various ways, mainly on the use, origin and destination of our money, it will be the governments that will exercise their powers of control, not the issuer of this digital money, which in Europe would be the ECB.

Governments would not only be able to see each and every movement of our digital wallets, they would also have the legal power to freeze, confiscate, collect current and future taxes, withhold certain funds, reverse transactions, effectively and immediately collect penalties for non-compliance with any regulation, they could also set an expiration date on the money received, prevent or limit savings on the pretext of promoting consumption and economic activity, as well as impose spending limits on products based on arbitrary criteria "always for our health" or based on our carbon footprint "to save the planet".

They could charge negative interest on their money, depending on each citizen's social score, according to an index of obedience called "social credit" that already exists in China.
"Negative interest" is a euphemism for a tax on savings; instead of rewarding savers' deposits with a certain amount of interest, they could be penalized with the aim of encouraging consumption and stimulating the economy.
Of course, in so-called "democratic" countries, this term will be changed to a friendlier name as an index of compliance with ESG criteria.

The acronym ESG stands for Environmental, Social and Governance factors, which are used by the World Economic Forum to assess the impact and responsibility of companies and individuals.

These criteria are increasingly being used to force companies to comply with the 2030 Agenda, also published by the World Economic Forum, or else the asset management giants will not provide investments if these factors are not met.

Several U.S. states have prohibited their respective public and state pension funds from investing in asset management funds that seek to impose these ESG criteria, as they have clearly proven to be counterproductive to the benefit of investors.

State attorneys from 19 states wrote a letter to Black Rock Company CEO Laurence D. Fink warning that BlackRock's ESG investment policies could be a "rampant violation" of the "single-interest rule," a legal principle that requires investment fiduciaries to act "to maximize financial return, not to promote social or political objectives."

References:
ESG investing becomes a lightning rod in American politics - CNA (channelnewsasia.com)

Conservative group takes anti-ESG campaign to the next level (axios.com)

The use of financial and economic coercion has become a political weapon, but historical experience shows that when the economy is driven by political rather than economic factors, it always ends in disaster.

Another possibility for the use of CBDC digital money would be to enforce "sanctions" against any product, brand, company or country that is designated as hostile by preventing transactions with a blacklist of individuals, companies or countries that the government deems "sanctioned". We must understand that the euphemistic term "sanction" really means boycott.

It will be particularly easy to block any transaction outside of the geographic area your government deems appropriate for you, thus restricting citizens to your zip code, city, region, or country, depending on the movement permissions you have been granted.

The new concept of "15-minute cities" is already emerging as a first step in Overton's time window.
Cities or neighborhoods where the average citizen should be able to meet all his or her needs without moving more than 15 minutes on foot or by bicycle, where the average car will be a luxury, thus saving energy to help "save the planet".
Overton's time window of 15-minute cities could be implemented like this:

Year one, this 2023.
The mass media of disinformation will tell you how good it would be for the planet to have commutes of no more than 15 minutes if you could satisfy all your needs in your neighborhood.

Year 2.
To save the planet, a small toll would be charged that would be automatically deducted from our CBDC wallet when your cell phone or car is detected beyond its 15-minute area of coverage from your residence.

In Spain, automatic vehicle identification systems are already being installed on the roads to pay the new road tax or toll, as was done in Portugal in the years following the 2008 crisis, to increase tax revenues to cover the unlimited public deficit and, incidentally, will be useful for controlling private and professional travel.

Let's keep in mind that the new mandatory safety device in the European Union, included in the emergency light that every vehicle must carry, will contain a SIM card for automatic transmission of geolocation data in case of accident or collision.

Of course, the traffic authorities have denied that this system will be used for this purpose.
Could this be a new "Overton window" for absolute control and geolocation?

If you are on foot, the default geolocation of your smartphone will transmit your position; if you leave your phone at home, it will be your vehicle that transmits your position.

When you use a CBDC smart card, the system records the physical location of use, and this geographic record can be used to monitor and track your movements.

The next twist will be when your own phone or car automatically sends a report to the authorities for speeding, since these devices can measure instantaneous speed.
We may think that this approach is a little bit paranoid, but the technical possibility is there, it is clear that it will be used for a greater safety of travel, of course.

Third year.
Since the reduction in the number of commutes expected by the government would not have been achieved, it will be necessary to request an administrative authorization, adequately justifying the cause of each trip beyond the distance of your 15-minute zone.

If you are identified by your phone, car, or use of your CBDC wallet outside your area, you will automatically be charged an ecological penalty for your environmental misconduct.
The penalty would increase with each offense.
Eventually, your driver's license would be revoked and your car, if you still have it, would be confiscated for the good of the planet.

This proposal of "15-minute cities", promoted by the new dogmas of the World Economic Forum itself, is actually nothing new, it is called Open Prison Regime, although there will always be time to turn it into a Closed Regime, a click would be enough to deactivate our CBDC wallets beyond those 15 minutes from our residence.

Time or calendar restrictions to use your money or buy certain products will also be possible and easy to implement.

The differences in economic and fiscal regulations and public deficits among the most indebted countries of the European Union will foreseeably lead to difficulties in monetary and fiscal management, which has recently been referred to as the "risk of European fragmentation".

Thus, the use of the CBDC control could easily be applied to create in practice what has been happening for years, especially during the serious debt crisis in Greece that threatened the unity of the European Union, a euro at "different speeds", once again a euphemistic expression to divide the euro, the single currency, into different currencies as needed, with fiscal rules and capital control, which although prohibited by the Treaty of the Union, would be easily implemented by governments or the European Commission.

This could mean that the Spanish euros in my Spanish CBDC application or wallet would not be freely usable in other European countries with a lower budget deficit or public debt, such as Germany or the Netherlands, and vice versa, without applying a corrective tax, i.e. the value of a Spanish digital euro would not necessarily have to be equal to that of a German digital euro, de facto destroying the monetary union.

In the event of a national bankruptcy of one of the member states of the European Union, a risk that is not only possible but highly probable, both the European Union and the national government in charge could easily, effectively and immediately confiscate our savings in our wallets in order to carry out a bail-in* or internal rescue at the national level.

This case is already foreseen, for example, in the Spanish law of "National Security", a term used by governments to legally execute any action that the rest of the laws do not allow, because invoking "National Security" all other legal precepts, rights and freedoms can be violated.

The technical possibilities for absolute control over citizens are of such a magnitude that they should make us think about whether we should submissively accept or resist CBDC digital currencies.

Obviously, this control will not be implemented immediately, but will wait for the definitive disappearance of cash in practice, or when cash is outlawed as being used only by criminals.
This situation could be precipitated in the event of international banking chaos or monetary reset, where CBDCs would undoubtedly be implemented.

In such a case, government control will be absolute.

Reference: Banking crisis accelerates the launch of FedNow and the digital dollar in the U.S.
Banking Crisis Potentially Accelerates CBDC Development In The U.S. - The Dales Report

The Federal Reserve announced the launch of FedNow, a 24/7 instant payment system, by July 2023.

The political war on cash is already well underway, especially in European countries like Spain, where it is illegal* to buy or sell anything over a thousand euros in cash..

* The Official State Gazette of July 10, 2021 published Law 11/2021 of July 9, 2021 on measures to prevent and combat tax fraud.

Likewise, it is mandatory to declare the movements in or out of Spain of amounts in cash equal to or greater than 10,000 euros. It is even mandatory to declare cash movements within Spain if the amount exceeds 100,000 euros.

Bank transfers over 10,000 euros must also be declared. This limit also applies to ATM withdrawals.

In order to declare these transfers, it is necessary to submit a form to the Tax Agency and provide documentation of both the person sending the transfer and the person receiving the money. It will also be necessary to "clarify the purpose" of the transfer.

Reference:
Tax Agency:Payment methods (agenciatributaria.gob.es)

We should ask ourselves, if my money is mine, why can I no longer pay anything over a thousand euros with legal tender? If my money is mine, why do I have to declare and explain to the government what I am doing with my money?

Fortunately, there are already citizens and states who have realized the danger:
Geneva, February 06, 2023. The Swiss will decide in a referendum whether it should be written into the law that the economy will never be completely virtual and that cash can always be used.

References:
Swiss to vote on initiative to keep cash in circulation - SWI swissinfo.ch
Switzerland's 'cash initiative' – what's at stake? - SWI swissinfo.ch

Legislation prohibiting the implementation of CBDC has been enacted in several U.S. states.

North Carolina House unanimously passes HB690: Banning Payments in #CBDC's & Prohibiting NC Participation in Any CBDC Testing.
The latest version of the legislation included limiting the Federal Reserve from using the U.S. state as a potential testing ground for its own CBDC pilot.
North Carolina House passes bill banning CBDC payments to the state (cointelegraph.com)

Florida Legislature passes Gov. DeSantis-backed ban on central bank digital currency.
The House passed SB 7054 by a 116-1 vote.
'With this bill, we are looking to protect the privacy of Floridians.'
Legislature passes Gov. DeSantis-backed ban on central bank digital currency — with Democratic support (floridapolitics.com)

As mentioned previously, it will not be necessary to ban cash in order to implement CBDCs, at least in the first years; their convenience and ease of use in replacing private means of payment will cause physical money to be no longer used in daily life.

Similarly, if several states pass laws against the implementation of CBDCs, promoted by the politicians of the day, it may not be very effective; an electoral change in the corresponding parliaments will be enough to repeal these laws.

But at least there is already a public and political reaction against the introduction of CBDCs.

CHAPTER 11.

More Money Stories.

Aware of the legitimate concerns raised by the introduction of CBDC currencies and the certain disappearance of cash, we should ask ourselves the following questions:

Can we avoid the introduction of digital currencies?

The short answer to this question is NO.
The possibilities of financial, economic and social control are such that political power can scarcely fail to seize them.

Can we delay the introduction of CBDC?

I am afraid not, as we have noted previously, 90% of the world's central banks are working quickly to implement central bank digital currencies.
The most likely timeline is: First public tests in the second half of 2023, initial deployment in 2024, and massive implementation in 2025.

Now in 2023, there are a handful of countries with CBDC digital currencies already in circulation, the two most important being Nigeria with its e-Naira and China with its e-CNY.

In Nigeria, the implementation of its CBDC, the e-Naira, can be described as disappointing. Africa's most populous country has experienced rapid socio-economic development despite having a political power that is "not very transparent". The e-Naira has a usage rate of only 0.5% due to the total mistrust of Nigerian citizens towards their government.

Adesoji Solanke, director at Renaissance Capital in Lagos, *told the media outlet, "The eNaira does not address any of* these basic use cases, so no surprise at its low adoption rates *so far,"*

Babatunde Obrimah, chief operating officer of the Fintech *Association of Nigeria, believes, "They [Younger Generation]* see the regulator as hostile to them and therefore have no *interest in anything it introduces,"*

Reference:
One Year on, Has E-Naira Defeated the Private Crypto Adoption? (beincrypto.com)

ABUJA, Nigeria (AP) — New clashes Tuesday between protesters and security forces in southern Nigeria left at least one person injured, amid demonstrations against a cash *shortage caused by the West African nation's push to rapidly* phase out its old currency notes.

Reference:
Protests over cash shortage as Nigeria banknote switch looms | AP News
"Rioters have attacked bank ATMs and blocked roads in three Nigerian cities as anger spilled on the streets over a scarcity *of cash"*

Reference:
Riots erupt in Nigerian cities as bank policy leads to scarcity of cash | Nigeria | The Guardian
By coincidence, Nigeria is one of the countries where bitcoin is most widely known and used to circumvent regulatory problems and the inefficiencies of banking and its physical currency.

About 35% of Nigerians used or owned bitcoin in early 2022.

The Nigerian government expects its national digital currency or CBDC, the eNaira, to receive more attention after a reduction in cash available at ATMs takes effect in a country where bitcoin is gaining followers.

A recent press release from the Central Bank of Nigeria (CBN) details that as of January 9, 2023, ATMs in the country will be allowed to withdraw a maximum of 20,000 naira per day, which is about $45.

Nigeria. The Central Bank of Nigeria limits cash withdrawals to a daily maximum of 42 euros in an attempt to boost electronic transactions through the use of its digital currency. Does the global trend to impose the use of central bank-controlled digital currencies, CBDC, endanger our freedoms?

Reference:
Nigeria wants to force the use of its CBDC - 11Onze

As we are already seeing, and will surely see in Europe, if the implementation and use of CBDC is not accepted or does not meet the governments' timetable, the coercive phase will begin, and the political power will have all the tools at its disposal to apply whatever force is necessary.

In the case of China, people used to obey the omnipotent power of government, perhaps due to the cultural bias of putting the common good before the personal good that distinguishes them from Western culture, the rate of acceptance has also been disappointing.

The People's Bank of China has released a report of its financial statistics that includes the digital yuan, or CBDC, in the metrics for the past 12 months.

According to this data, the central bank has indicated that there were 13.61 billion digital yuan ($2 billion) in circulation at the end of 2022, an increase of 15.3% from the previous year.

Despite this increase, it represents only 0.13% of the total fiat currency in circulation. The Financial Statistics 2022 report notes that the digital yuan in circulation did not cause any "notable changes" in the data.

Reference:
China's central bank includes digital yuan in report on currency circulation (cointelegraph.com)

The reason for the low usage rate of the digital yuan is mainly due to the fact that digital phone payments have already been massively implemented in China through the popular payment applications of AliPay, a company of the electronic giant Alibaba, and WeChat, the most popular instant messaging application in China.

These applications are so popular and widely used that they are practically the preferred method of payment, and as I mentioned in Chapter One, the first question that users will ask when it comes to implementing CBDC currencies is, "What advantage will CBDCs give me over the electronic systems I already use?"

For this reason, and also because these companies were entering the financial market by offering quick loans over the phone without actually being banks, the Chinese government decided to curb their business activities with strict measures.

These Chinese tech giants have advantages because they have all the information and therefore the credit risk assessment of their customers and could use the money deposited by their users in their payment applications to grant loans using the well-known fractional reserve technique.

Banks will face stiff competition from WeChat alone, which has 900 million daily users in China and 1.2 billion worldwide.

In November 2020, Alibaba-owned Ant Financial was set to go public in Shanghai in what would have been the largest IPO in history, but its permit was revoked.

It appears that it could reapply for the largest IPO, which is the formal, regulated process for a company to start selling its shares on the stock exchange, as early as 2023.

The big tech companies have long wanted to get into the financial business, especially Amazon, Google and Apple.

It is known that Google has a banking license in Lithuania, which would give it access to the entire European Union, and several other licenses as a payment institution, for example in Ireland.

With this new license, Google Payment Ireland will be able to manage credit cards, perform online money transfers for users and foreign exchange transactions.

It will also be able to provide customers with detailed analysis of their spending patterns to create customized financial and budgeting plans based on the information in its databases.

Apple and Amazon also hold banking licenses in the European Union that allow them to operate as banks throughout the Union.

These companies have the capital, all the information about their users, and the corporate image to become a competitor that could easily cannibalize the entire European banking industry, time will tell.

I must confess that I am a customer of the three technology companies mentioned, and from a user's point of view, each of them gives me more confidence than any of the European banks.

Undoubtedly, the banking business is besieged by several possible enemies, not only the CBDCs, but also the technology giants, all of which already have very convenient and popular payment platforms for their users.

Knowing the likely problems of CBDCs and being familiar with payment platforms such as Google Pay, Apple Pay or Samsung Pay, what advantages can the central bank offer us?

After all, goods and services must compete, and only the most efficient and convenient will succeed, and CBDCs will have to compete not only with payment companies, technology, traditional banks, and fintech or neo-banks, but also with each other.

The centralized political power will find some excuse to ban EU citizens from using the Digital Yuan or Digital Ruble, or at least they will try.

But what excuse could they find to boycott the Digital Dollar, the Digital Pound or the Digital Swiss Franc?

"Don't put all your eggs in one basket" is the first rule of good financial practice.

Other Money Stories.

The neocolonial "seigniorage" of the CFA franc.

For 75 years, the CFA franc has been the currency of fourteen African countries, almost all former French colonies, and is itself divided into two, for West Africa (XOF) and for Central Africa (XAF).

Namely: Benin, Burkina Faso, Côte d'Ivoire, Guinea-Bissau, Mali, Niger, Senegal and Togo in West Africa; and Cameroon, Central African Republic, Chad, Republic of the Congo, Equatorial Guinea and Gabon in Central Africa.

The acronym of this currency stands for "African Financial Community", although at the time of its creation it stood for "French Community of Africa".

It should be noted that in April 2022, the Central African Republic declared bitcoin as legal tender alongside the CFA franc.

This is the second country to do so after El Salvador, which made bitcoin legal tender in September 2021.

In its origins, the CFA Franc was a colonial currency imposed by the metropolis, and even today Paris retains a great deal of influence over the countries that use it.

This currency is issued by the Bank of France and has a fixed exchange rate with the currency used by France, first the franc and now the euro.

In order to use this currency, the central banks of these countries must keep 50% of their reserves with the French Treasury, they are also obliged to buy French public debt, and the Bank of France has a virtual veto over the monetary policy decisions of the central banks of these countries.

There is an international controversy about France's policy of neo-colonialism towards its former colonies, which is growing with time.

It is not difficult to imagine that the growing influence of China throughout Africa, on the one hand, and the rejection of the former metropolis, on the other, will turn these countries into fertile ground for the massive use of the digital yuan, with the de facto disappearance of the already decadent currency, the CFA franc.

References:

What is the CFA Franc and which countries use it?

CFA Franc | History and information | BCEAO.

Franco CFA.

CFA franc - Wikipedia

The model and operation of the CFA Franc is a clear practical example of how the issuer of a fiat currency acquires enormous power, which many economists and analysts describe as a Ponzi scheme* or neo-feudalism.
We have addressed the dangers associated with CBDCs, such as absolute control over citizens and the economy, as well as possible restrictions on freedoms, but the most basic danger is simply that a CBDC not only reinforces the worst political control of society, but also remains a fiat currency.

We already know that a fiat currency is backed by nothing, its issuance has no limit, so its value tends to zero.
All fiat currencies end their life cycle with a monetary reset.

A monetary or currency reset is a process in which a new currency is introduced to replace the existing one, usually in times of deep financial and social crisis.
It usually occurs when the public has lost confidence in the currency, causing the exchange rate to fall, or when a country is experiencing hyperinflation and/or bankruptcy.

The cause of a failing currency is often related to government over-indebtedness and the perception that the government has lost the ability to pay what it owes. Reading the above, we can realize that the mentioned circumstances are so common to all countries and fiat currencies today that they lead us to believe that a collapse of the fiat monetary system is not too far away.

This perception, coupled with excessive spending and an apparent inability to raise taxes that are already strangling individual, corporate and national economies, can lead to a loss of confidence in the currency and make a reset more likely.

Currency reset processes vary from time to time, but generally involve exchanging the old currency for a new one. People may be allowed to exchange some of their old bank notes for new ones, or for CBDC up to a certain limit, as will bank balances; rarely will it be 1:1, especially for large balances, which is effectively a confiscation of wealth.

During monetary reset crises, corporations may also be treated "differently" from individuals. Special rules may apply to certain types of institutions, such as banks, pension funds, foreign governments, international institutions, government agencies, and the government itself.

Bonds* and money market funds* may not be converted because they make up the bulk of the debt that the failed currency cannot repay.

Corporate bonds, mortgages, loans, and private debt can remain in the old currency or be converted to the new, often with "elastic" rules tailored to the financial sector and the political and ruling power.

The new currency will come with the "guaranteed" promise that it is tied to something of value, and "safeguards" will be promised to ensure that the loss of value seen in the previous failed currency will never happen again.

Observing the growing geopolitical tensions between the Western countries on one hand and the BRICS group of countries on the other, it seems obvious that we are heading towards an economic fragmentation that will eventually affect the global monetary system to form a new map of what is beginning to be called a multipolar world, as opposed to the current unipolar world led by the United States.

In the Western countries, we will include the United States, all the countries of Western Europe, Canada, Australia, New Zealand, South Korea and Japan. We would be talking about less than 1 billion people.

In the BRICS, the acronym for the founding countries, we will include Brazil, Russia, India, China, South Africa.
But there is a long list of candidates to join the founding group, including: Saudi Arabia, Qatar, Kuwait, Bahrain, United Arab Emirates, Argentina, Iran, Egypt and Algeria.

Observe that the BRICS will include China as the world's factory, the largest producers of oil, energy and raw materials, as well as giants in agri-food production.
Just add China with 1.4 billion people, India with another 1.4 billion, the Muslim world with 1.8 billion, plus 260 million from Brazil and Argentina, almost five times the population of the Western countries.

These countries have commodities, manufacturing, and economies with great potential, and large populations with young age indexes, in contrast to Western countries, especially Europe and Japan, which are already facing population aging problems due to low birth rates.

Reference:
Economic power shift: BRICS nations overtake G7 in global GDP (Purchasing Power Parity).
Economic Power Shift: BRICS Nations Outpace G7 in Global GDP (thenewscrypto.com)

The BRICS nations, Brazil, Russia, India, China and South Africa, have surpassed the G7 nations in economic power.
In terms of purchasing power parity (PPP), these nations rank first and form the world's largest gross domestic product (GDP) bloc.

The GDP Purchasing Power Parity (PPP) economic index is an economic indicator used to compare the standard of living between different countries, taking into account the Gross

Domestic Product (GDP) per capita in relation to the cost of living in each country.

This index is the set of final goods and services produced in a country during a year, but instead of using the prices of that country, it uses the prices of the United States, which will serve as the basis of calculation for all countries..

The current unipolar world, led by the United States since the Second World War, is based on an intact industrial position after the Second World War, which has kept the United States in a privileged position by imposing its currency, the dollar, as the currency of international trade and world reserve.

As Charles de Gaulle said in his famous speech mentioned in chapter 7:
"The fact that many countries accept as a matter of principle that dollars are as good as gold means that Americans are borrowing for free at the expense of other countries. For what the U.S. owes, it pays, at least in part, with money that only it can issue.
We consider it necessary that international trade should be based on an indisputable monetary standard, and that it should not bear the stamp of any particular country."

These words are undoubtedly enlightening, because if we analyze the public debt, which is very high worldwide, but absolutely unsustainable in Western countries, with the United States leading the way with almost 32 trillion and a debt/GDP ratio of 128% in 2022, the same debt/GDP ratio will reach 100% in Europe and 259% in Japan.

We could assume that Western countries, including Japan, are in fact sustaining the economy thanks to a constant issuance of money, which devalues our currencies.

The case of Japan stands out in every index we can analyze. Over the past decade, the Bank of Japan (BoJ) has managed to gobble up 80% of Japan's exchange-traded funds (ETFs), which represent about 7% of the country's $6 trillion stock market, as well as 40% of all government debt.

Reference:
How much of the Japanese stock market is held by the BoJ. BlackBull Markets (blackbullmarkets.com)
https://blackbullmarkets.com/en/market-reviews/how-much-of-the-japanese-stock-market-does-the-boj-own/

But this process has accelerated over the past decade.
Japan's massive government debt is being bought almost entirely by the Bank of Japan, or in simple terms, all of Japan's gigantic government debt is being bought with new money created by the Bank of Japan, and this situation has led Japan to the highest rate of inflation and the largest decline in the value of the yen against the dollar in 32 years. If our economy is sustained by the constant creation of money out of thin air, there will be a loss of confidence and a monetary reset will be inevitable.

The BRICS countries, led by Russia and China, are already working on a new international currency that will most likely be backed by their gold and commodity reserves, as both are also the largest gold producers.

If this currency is used and backed by the economic bloc with the largest population and the largest production of commodities, it could quickly displace the dollar as the international trade and reserve currency, causing serious problems for Western countries.

However, this new currency will have to meet the first requirement of money, which is to be generally accepted, a quality that is always linked to trust.

International trade in national currencies always raises the problem of trust. If a nation issues unlimited amounts of money to buy services and tangible goods or commodities, the exporting nation will eventually realize that it is delivering tangible value in exchange for colored numbers.

The United States' strategy of using the dollar as a weapon, sanctioning political or economic rivals, and confiscating their dollar reserves, which are nothing more than accounting entries in the banks, has already made the rest of the countries aware that the dollar is not a reliable currency, because it can be created out of nothing in unlimited quantities, and it can also be confiscated at the will of its issuer.

The renowned American investor Ray Dalio analyzes in his successful book "Principles for Confronting the New World Order: Why Nations Succeed and Fail," and it is not my wish to spoil this great book, which I recommend, the cycles that have been repeated throughout history of the rise and fall of dominant nations.
These historical cycles present analogies as, for various reasons that Dalio explains in his book, a nation manages to rise with a hegemony that soon moves to its currency, which becomes the standard for world trade and reserve currency.
This fact, as Charles de Gaulle also describes in his previously mentioned speech, leads the hegemonic state to an exorbitant privilege that allows it to go into debt for free, which usually strengthens its hegemony, although this

inevitably ends in inflation due to the issuance of money to finance this debt, as well as its military power.

The current geopolitical circumstances indicate that the decline of the United States has already begun, with growing social tensions, given the huge social gap between the rich and the poor, a totally disproportionate debt that is already unpayable, and has entered into a spiral of creating new money to sustain its economy and pay the interest on the debt previously created, which can only be paid with new money, which further inflates the debt.

I invite the reader to visit this Internet link: US Debt Clock. https://www.usdebtclock.org/world-debt-clock.html

On this website you can see in real time the debt of the most important countries in the world, but let's look not only at the first column of public debt, but also at the following ones: Gross Domestic Product; Debt to Gross Domestic Product Ratio; and in the last column, Debt in the hands of International Creditors to GDP Ratio.
United States: 31.5 trillion debt, GDP: 26 trillion, debt/GDP ratio: 94%, foreign-owned debt/GDP ratio: 93%, foreign-owned debt/GDP ratio: 93%.

The next countries on the list show very similar data, although the ratio of foreign-owned debt to GDP is considerably lower in the cases of China at 17%, India at 25%, and Russia with the best debt/GDP ratio in the world at only 19% and a foreign-owned debt/GDP ratio of 26%.
Note that all three are founding members of the international BRICS group.

What we can observe in the debt data leaves no room for doubt: The fiat money monetary system, based on the constant issuance of money, is doomed to implode.

It is highly probable that we are heading towards a multipolar world, currently projected by the BRICS and their current candidates, which could establish an international electronic currency backed by gold and commodities, and the other pole, known by the Western countries plus Korea and Japan, with a monetary system on the verge of imploding and based on the infinite creation of money backed by really nothing.

This would lead to a systemic and worldwide economic and social crisis, which would necessarily entail a monetary reset of the hegemonic currency and the establishment of a new world and monetary order.

Remember that most of the reserves of the world's countries, especially those most closely tied to the United States, are denominated in dollars; if the dollar loses its status as the world's reserve currency, this collateral represented by the reserves will be worthless enough to support other national currencies or the European Union's euro.

The boom-and-bust cycles of the hegemonic countries analyzed by Ray Dalio occur over considerable periods of time, but we can find other economic cycles that are shorter in time, which we could call cyclical and non-systemic booms and busts like those mentioned by Ray Dalio.

These cycles, of which this author has seen several, occur every few years, and all of them, although they occur under different circumstances and seem to have different causes, always have one element in common.

When central banks increase the money supply by expanding credit and debt, an economic boom occurs, which also creates inflation. This process is called Quantitative Easing.

When this debt and inflation reach certain limits, or for whatever reason, the central banks reduce the money supply by raising interest rates and withdrawing money from circulation, this process is called Quantitative Tightening, a recession with high unemployment and economic crisis ensues.
Then, as a supposed response to this crisis, the central banks begin to expand the monetary mass again, increasing credit again by lowering interest rates, and the periodic cycles of monetary expansion and contraction of credit and debt are repeated.

Those who have conserved their liquidity during the crisis or those who have easy access to credit in a new phase of monetary expansion, such as commercial banks, rapidly increase their wealth by buying companies and assets at low cost as a consequence of the previous crisis.

This process is called the "Cantillon Effect", which is explained in economist Richard Cantillon's theory of the unequal impact of monetary policy on the economy.
It is a phenomenon whereby the issuance of money by central banks benefits those who print money to the detriment of the general population, because the newly created money is neither simultaneously nor evenly distributed throughout the population.
The process of monetary expansion therefore involves a transfer of wealth.

Some may argue that the actions of central banks are intended to counteract economic boom and bust cycles.
In the opinion of this author and many analysts, the opposite is true: it is the intervention of central banks in economic policy that creates boom and bust cycles in the economy.

This was supposedly the premise for which central banks were created, to fight cyclical crises.
If we analyze history, we will see that this excuse is false.

CBDCs are presented to the public on several premises publicized by governments and central banks, such as that they are a new form of the same money we already use, that they will not replace physical money, and that they will be more convenient, interchangeable for goods and services as well as for bank notes and physical money.

Throughout this book I have tried to sow more than reasonable doubt about the veracity of these premises.

This author believes that the fiat monetary system, based on the issuance of money with no backing nor limit, to pay a debt that is also growing without limit, will lead to a loss of value and confidence that this debt can be repaid, which will inexorably lead to a monetary reset.

On March 9, 2023, the small U.S. bank Silver Gate Bank declared bankruptcy.

The next day, on March 10, 2023, the mid-sized Silicon Valley Bank also failed, and the FDIC or Bank Deposit Insurance Corporation of the United States intervened.

This second bank to fail within 48 hours triggered a widespread banking panic not only in the United States, but also in Europe.

On March 14, 2023, Signature Bank also failed.

This forced the Federal Reserve and the U.S. Treasury to take immediate and drastic measures to prevent a general banking collapse.

The reason for the collapse of these banks is the same as almost always, fractional reserve banking, where banks keep only a very small percentage of their customers' deposits available for withdrawal while they lend the rest to other customers or invest in assets that provide them with profitability, hoping that many of the depositing customers will not want to withdraw their money at the same time.

Due to the lack of confidence in Silicon Valley Bank, customers withdrew 42,000 million in the morning of the day of its failure.

We must understand that a bank, by definition, is always an insolvent entity, and this assertion is not an overstatement.

The raw material with which a bank works is the money of its creditors, i.e. its depositors, as well as other entities, including the central bank, which "lend" it money so that the bank can make profits by investing in various financial assets and granting loans.

That is, using its liabilities or money owed to its depositors and other entities, it makes profits with medium and long-term assets and repays the loans it has made with interest.

In a normal situation, all may go well, since generally not many depositors come to withdraw their deposits at the same time.

The fractional reserve system on which banking is based is essentially a fraud, because when a bank lends capital to a customer who asks for a loan, the bank is really pretending to use the deposits of other customers, but without reflecting that capital taken from the depositors' accounts.
Depositors still see 100% of their deposits in their account balance and can withdraw those funds today.

Since banks invest most of their deposits in medium- and long-term assets, they will not be able to cope with a massive withdrawal of their depositors in the short term.
Lack of confidence always triggers this reaction
In a situation of banking panic with massive customer withdrawals, banks can liquidate short-term assets such as stocks or government bonds in the secondary market or by borrowing from the central bank using the medium- and long-term assets they hold as collateral.

This happened to the three failed banks mentioned above and threatened a large number of other small and medium-sized regional banks.
In an attempt to obtain liquidity, Silicon Valley Bank sold shares that had been devalued in the stock market in recent months, and also sold its treasury bonds in the secondary market at a huge loss, as they had fallen in price.

The reader will ask: If U.S. Treasury Bonds are Fixed interest rate assets*, and are the safest, and most liquid assets, how can they lose value?

The answer is not difficult to understand, during the decade and a half after the collapse of 2008, interest rates have been close to zero in the United States, and negative in Europe, so Treasury Bonds issued during those years, and we are talking about an overwhelming money supply, had a very low yield between 1% and 2%.

As the Federal Reserve has initiated a steep rise in interest rates reaching in the United States at the time of writing this book the yield on bonds at 3.75%, the new bonds issued are now much more profitable than the bonds issued in previous years.

Bonds are fixed interest assets only if they are held until maturity; if you want to sell or liquidate them before maturity, you have to go to the secondary market* where they are traded according to supply and demand.

Obviously, investors will prefer to invest in recently issued bonds with an interest rate or yield close to 4%, rather than in bonds from previous years with a yield of 1%.
Therefore, the market will assign a lower value to bonds with lower yields, and if you want to sell them, you will have to accept a drop in price at least equal to what the investor will lose compared to buying a newer bond.

All banks, large and small, have in their balance sheet, or in their list of assets a huge amount of money, some of it in stocks and most of it in fixed interest securities, mainly US Treasury bonds, as the safest and most liquid asset that exists, but let's not forget that in just 18 months, during 2020 and the first half of 2021, the US Federal Reserve will have issued 25% of all the dollars created in the history of the dollar, this huge amount of money supply would necessarily have to generate an inflationary event like the one we are experiencing.

With the banks' balance sheets full of bonds with very low profitability compared to the current bonds, the market logically assigns them a value much lower than the purchase value, known as unrealized losses, the banks can wait for the maturity period according to the composition of their bond portfolio to receive at the end of that period 100% of the nominal value of these bonds, but if for some reason they are forced to sell them before maturity, they will suffer catastrophic losses.

This happened to Silicon Valley Bank, after selling the bonds it could at a loss, it tried to increase its capital, but when it did not find new investors to provide more capital to the bank, it caused panic among its depositors, who began a massive withdrawal of funds, leading to the bank's bankruptcy and its intervention by the FDIC, or Bank Deposit Insurance Corporation of the United States.

The following banks, Signature Bank and First Republic Bank, suffered identical circumstances, so the Federal Reserve and the Treasury decided to intervene once again to prevent the banking panic from spreading throughout the banking system.

The solution? Simple, the same as always, inject new money and manipulate the markets with increasingly extreme practices that will end up undermining the confidence of investors and citizens.

Since all the banks have an enormous mass of money in devalued Treasury bonds, the "happy" idea that the regulators and the Treasury have come up with is to value the banks' bond reserves not at the real market price, but at the nominal price, or maturity price.

And on the basis of this "falsely valued" collateral, they will issue 300 billion in new money, which they will lend to the troubled banks on favorable terms.

The situation of the big banks is not much different, their balance sheets are accumulating huge unrealized losses because they have not had to sell these bonds for the moment, with the new injection of liquidity they will probably not have to do so anymore.

We should ask ourselves some questions here.
If 300 billion was issued to save three banks, how much would be needed if more than a hundred regional banks needed it?

Reference:
More than 186 U.S. banks are at risk of collapse, analysis shows.
https://papers.ssrn.com/sol3/papers.cfm?abstract_id=4387676

Is it a good idea to bail out a mismanaged bank with public money or funds that will end up devaluing our money?
The reasons to condemn bank bailouts would be enough to write another book.
In Europe, the giant Swiss bank Credit Suisse, classified as a global systemic risk, was on the verge of bankruptcy, and the Swiss National Bank (SNB) has decided to inject 54 billion to avoid its immediate bankruptcy.

We should know that the SNB itself has accumulated losses of 133 billion in 2022, and now in 2023 it has already committed 54 billion more to try to save Credit Suisse.
Finally, on Monday, March 20, before the opening of the markets in the West, the purchase of Credit Suisse by its

competitor UBS, for about 3 billion, with the support, if necessary, and the author fears it will be necessary, of 100 billion, which would be provided by the Swiss National Bank, known by its acronym SNB, is announced.

In anticipation of 10,000 layoffs, UBS is taking over about 5 billion of Credit Suisse's known losses and valuing the bonds issued by Credit Suisse at zero.
This will result in terrible losses for its investors, especially the Saudi National Bank, whose investment portfolio has literally propped up Credit Suisse for at least the last few years.
It may be history by the time you read this book, or rather the beginning of a new story of the failure of the international monetary and financial system.

Reference: Swiss National Bank posts record $143 billion loss (cnbc.com)

The 2022 loss means the central bank will not make its usual payout to Switzerland's central and regional governments.
Last year, the SNB paid out 6 billion francs.

The purchase of Credit Suisse by UBS and the support of the Swiss National Bank may initially be enough for the combined entity to meet its short-term obligations, but it will certainly not be enough to restore the confidence of clients and depositors.

As we have said before, banks are by definition insolvent companies, their assets are for the medium and long term, but their obligations to their creditors could be immediate in the event of a lack of confidence and panic.

Let's take a look at these data published by Mises Institute on its website: https://mises.org

Reference: Central Banks: Profligacy in Lockstep.
https://mises.org/wire/central-banks-profligacy-lockstep

Numbers to get your attention!

The Swiss National Bank's (SNB) financial statements for the nine months ending September 30, 2022, show a bottom-line loss of US$150 billion.
Still, the SNB has a capital ratio, a bank's equity to its total assets, over 6%.

In contrast, the Federal Reserve's reported capital ratio, which does not reflect the Fed's massive mark-to-market losses, is 0.5%. The Federal Reserve Bank of New York, by far the largest of the Federal Reserve Banks, has a reported capital ratio of 0.3%, again not counting its market value losses.

The Reserve Bank of Australia announced in September that losses on its investments caused its capital to drop to a negative $8 billion on June 30.

The Bank of England joined "the club of major central banks showing negative net worth" if its investments are marked-to-market, *Grant's Interest Rate Observer* reported. Thus far, the Bank has lost $230 billion on its bond investments, 33 times the Bank's capital of $7 billion as of February 2022, its fiscal year-end.
Fortunately for the Bank, it has an indemnity from His *Majesty's Treasury, that is, the taxpayers, to cover the losses.*

The Bank of Canada carries most of its investments at market value, and its financial statements reflect market value losses of $26 billion as of November 2022

Our monetary system is based on fiat currency, which is essentially debt created out of thin air.
This system has led to a situation where there is always more debt than actual money in circulation, making it inherently unstable and prone to collapse.

Furthermore, our economy relies heavily on a banking system that is inherently insolvent and is kept afloat only by waning public confidence.

This leaves us vulnerable to financial crises and underscores the need for systemic reform to ensure greater long-term stability and sustainability.

The geopolitical shift from unipolar, led by the United States and its dollar, to multipolar, where the majority of the world's population no longer trusts the dollar and is building a new international trade currency backed by commodities and tangible goods, seems to indicate that we are accelerating toward a monetary reset.

And this makes me fear that the "final solution" will be the introduction of CBDCs, a dystopian system in which your money, your savings and your assets will no longer belong to you.
You will only be allowed to use them according to the impositions of central bankers and political power.

Alternatives.

Gary Gensler, currently the 2023 Chairman of the Securities and Exchange Commission (SEC), the official regulator of the securities market in the United States, has publicly stated on several occasions that in his opinion all cryptocurrencies except Bitcoin are securities, an opinion with which this author fully agrees.

In order to determine what is a market value, the Howey test is used.
The Howey test refers to U.S. Supreme Court case law used to determine whether a transaction can be considered an "investment contract" and therefore a security that should be subject to the disclosure and registration requirements of the Securities Act of 1933 and the Securities Exchange Act of 1934.

To this end, the U.S. Supreme Court has established four criteria for determining whether an investment contract exists.

An investment contract requires:
An investment of money.
In a common enterprise.
With an expectation of profit.
Derived from the efforts of others.

In June 2018, former SEC Chairman Jay Clayton specifically clarified that bitcoin is not a security.

"These are replacements for sovereign currencies, replace the dollar, the euro, the yen with bitcoin," Clayton said. "That type of currency is not a security."

Reference:
SEC Chairman Clayton says agency won't change definition of a security (cnbc.com)

Bitcoin has never sought public funding, i.e. from any company, to develop its technology, and it does not pass the Howey test used by the SEC to classify securities.

All other cryptocurrencies, also known as altcoins ("alt" for alternatives to bitcoin), may have some value depending on their usefulness in efficiently solving some purpose, and all of them, except bitcoin, have an organization or company behind them.
All altcoins meet the criteria of the Howey test.

Therefore, we can be sure that it is only a matter of time before U.S. regulators take legal action against all cryptocurrencies; all except bitcoin.
Bitcoin is really in the same category as a commodity*, i.e. a good, product or raw material, such as gold.

Bitcoin could solve all monetary problems, including inflation, lack of trust between parties to be used in international trade, and the growth since its creation in 2009 is astounding.

Unlike fiat money, which is created as debt, every unit of euro, dollar or yen we own is someone's debt, bitcoin is no one's debt.

Bitcoin has a finite, limited and public-known issuance of 21 million units, of which 19 million have already been mined.
Its value against some fiat currencies may still be extremely volatile in the short to medium term, but as the New York Fed's publication acknowledges. Paper NO. 1052 of February

2023. mentioned above, it has an average annual growth rate over the entire sample (last 10 years) of 220% per year due to its recent decline (in 2021).

Since its launch, Bitcoin has suffered all kinds of cyber-attacks on its network of nodes, media attacks and regulatory attacks, by governments and economic authorities, nothing has been able to stop its blockchain.

On February 10, 2011, it reached the price of 1 dollar, today, March 2023, it exceeds 28,000 dollars per unit.

Bitcoin's massive decentralization makes it unstoppable, censorship-resistant, unconfiscable and its transactions immutable.

Bitcoin allows transactions between two parties without the need for mutual trust and without any intermediary or central authority, and has been operating without interruption since its inception in 2009.

Bitcoin, its protocol, and its blockchain cannot be controlled or altered by any government, corporation, group, or individual.
Bitcoin's characteristics make it the best money yet created, especially for Internet commerce.
It is possible that over time, nations will discover that it could be the ideal solution for settlement and payment in international trade, including trade between political enemies.

Of course, it will be rejected by governments, as its widespread use would cause them to lose control over fiat currencies, but they could quickly accept it for international trade, as Russia and Iran, among other states, are already exploring.

By 2023, there are already two states, El Salvador and the Central African Republic, that grant bitcoin legal tender status, along with the dollar in El Salvador and the CFA franc in the Central African Republic.

The state control that will be exercised through CBDC currencies will force citizens to consider a monetary alternative in defense of freedom, our money and our patrimony.

We should keep in mind the concept that when money is nothing more than a record in a computer system controlled by the government, it will no longer be our money, we will have permission to use it, permission that can be conditioned or revoked at any time.

Again, to quote Charles de Gaulle's speech in which he said, "We think it necessary that international trade should be based on an indisputable monetary standard, and that it should not bear the stamp of a particular country. What standard? The truth is that no standard other than gold is conceivable!

Charles de Gaulle could not imagine any standard other than the gold standard, because at that time the Internet could not even be imagined.

I cannot miss this opportunity to recommend the book:
The Bitcoin Standard: The Decentralized Alternative to Central Banking.By professor Saifedean Ammous. Professor of Economics at the Adnan Kassar School of Business at the American University of Lebanon.

Thanks to "my age", I've been fortunate enough to witness several significant societal changes resulting from the advancements in technology.

I have always been a technology enthusiast, and since my teenage years I have witnessed firsthand the evolution of computing and the popularization of microcomputing in the 80's of the last century, which later became my profession.
I enjoyed living through this revolution, and in those years, with my 8-bit personal computers that could barely display 256 colors, I was already dreaming of digital photography and audio.

I still remember the comments of professional photographers at the time who argued that poor digital photography would never compete with, much less replace, analog photography based on chemical film.

There is a famous conversation at a Kodak board meeting when one of the attendees suggested promoting the incipient digital photography that Kodak was already developing.

And the response to that suggestion was:
"If digital photography develops, what will we do with our entire industrial base of chemical film and photographic paper production?"
"Filmless photography is nice, but don't tell anyone about it."

Failure to innovate was the primary reason for Kodak's demise with the advent of digital photography.
Although the company essentially invented the digital camera, it suppressed the technology out of fear that it would threaten its profits from traditional film.

Digitalization, like all previous technological revolutions, has been disruptive in all areas, and although it is still being resisted in the monetary system, it will be no different.
And no, when I talk about digital money, I am not talking about credit cards or Google/Apple Pay.

I also remember the introduction of the Internet into every home, with modems plugged into the phone's audio line, the first emails sent from the Netscape browser, and the first songs in mp3 format.

Things that were unimaginable just a few years earlier became normal thanks to personal computers and the Internet.

I remember, when I was a student of digital electronics and microprocessors in the late 1980s, that I read with some skepticism in an electronics magazine that standards were being developed for cellular telephony and that in a few years we would be able to make phone calls from our cars.

A few years later, smartphones with permanent Internet connection would arrive. The technological evolution forces changes in our lives and in our society, it has always been like that, since the time of the caves, what happens now is that these changes are accelerated, more and more important and in less time.

With these experiences in mind, I can safely say that it won't be long before we have a universal and neutral digital money, free from government and corporate interference, impossible to confiscate, and impossible to be censored. What's even more, it may already be available and accessible to everyone.

The idea that government and corporate fiat money can be replaced by a different monetary system may still seem like utopia or fiction, but it is not, this technology already exists.

"Any sufficiently advanced technology is indistinguishable *from magic*"
Arthur C. Clarke.

Glossary.

Accounting entry.

A written entry detailing a commercial or economic movement that changes the assets of a person or company. In accounting, journal entries are used to record each of a company's transactions.

Backing.

Backing, in finance, is a guarantee offered or received to support a financial transaction.

For example, in a mortgage, the guarantee or financial backing provided as collateral is the property.

During the Gold Standard period, the backing of banknotes was a certain amount of gold for which the banknote could be redeemed.

Bail-in / Bail-out.

Bail-in, or more simply a financial rescue, is the refinancing of a troubled financial institution or entity.

Bail-out refers to the fact that the capital for this rescue comes from outside the entity, usually from other entities or from the states, which will pass this cost on to the taxpayers.

Bail-out was the model used in the 2008 financial crisis.

Bail-in refers to the fact that the capital to rescue the troubled institution comes from within the institution, i.e. from shareholders or depositors.

After the 2008 crisis, all the countries of the world updated their laws in order to carry out bail-ins in future crises.

It is very important to understand that in the future, when a bank is in trouble, the authorities will enforce these laws by taking capital from the bank's creditors, i.e. its shareholders and depositors, and only after that, if it is still not enough, the deposit guarantee funds will act.

Balance Sheet.

Balance sheet is a financial report that is made periodically; monthly, quarterly or annually, detailing all the assets, value of what is owned, and liabilities or debts and the resulting capital of a company.

With a very simple formula:

Assets - Liabilities (Or debts) = Capital of the company.

This term is commonly used in the media to refer to financial assets that have been "purchased" by central banks, such as corporate bonds, government bonds, or treasury bonds.

Note that these assets are purchased with new money created out of thin air to make such purchases.

Central banks are creating new money with these purchases.

Bear Market / Bull Market.

Colloquial expressions of financial terminology to denote a bear market, or Bear Market, in analogy to how the bears attack, from top to bottom, when lowering their claws, or Bull Market, Bull Market, in analogy to how the bulls attack, goring from bottom to top.

BETA Index.

In financial terminology, the beta index is an indicator that measures the volatility of an asset (a stock or security) relative to the market in which it is traded.

For example, if a stock's beta index is 1.5, it means that if the market goes up 1%, the stock will go up 1.5%, and if the market goes down 1%, the stock will go down 1.5%.

In this way, the beta index serves to measure the relative risk of an asset compared to the behavior of other similar assets within the same market.

BIS (Bank for International Settlements).

The Bank for International Settlements (BIS) is an international organization dedicated to promoting monetary and financial cooperation among central banks and other monetary authorities. Founded in 1930 and headquartered in Basel, Switzerland, the BIS is the central bank of central banks and serves as a forum for discussion and coordination on issues related to global financial stability.

The BIS focuses on three main areas of work: economic research and analysis, international monetary and financial cooperation, and services to central banks and other monetary authorities

Bitcoin.

Bitcoin is a decentralized, intermediary-free digital currency.

It allows online payments to be sent directly between parties without going through a financial institution.

It is based on a network of computers that verify and record transactions in a public ledger called a blockchain.

Bitcoin can be sent and received over the Internet without the need to trust any entity or authority.

Its issuance is limited to 21 million units, of which 19 million have been issued, and the rest will be issued in a decreasing mode until the 21 million are completed around the year 2140.

Blockchain.

Usually used to refer to the Bitcoin ledger.

Blockchain is a database technology that enables the creation and management of a digital ledger in which transactions involving a currency or asset are recorded and verified.

Each transaction is grouped into a block that is cryptographically linked to the previous block, forming a blockchain.

This blockchain is shared and updated by all network participants without the need for a central authority.

Blockchain guarantees security through decentralization in multiple nodes, distribution of the database in multiple locations, as well as transparency, traceability and immutability of operations, since data is encrypted and cannot be modified or deleted.

Bond.

A bond is a type of loan that a person makes to a company or government. The issuer of the bond undertakes to repay the money borrowed within a specified period of time, plus interest, which may be fixed or variable according to a predetermined rate.

In financial terms, a bond can also be called a debt security, debt financial asset or fixed income instrument, since its formalization establishes an interest rate that the issuer will pay to the investor.

There are short-, medium- and long-term bonds, months, 1 year, 5, 10, 30 years.

During the period or duration of a bond, especially medium- and long-term bonds, they can be traded in the secondary market.

For example, if an investor buys a 10-year government bond paying 4% interest annually, the investor will receive 4% each year from the issuer, and at the end of the term or maturity, the issuer will return the last year's interest plus the total (or nominal) amount of the bond.

But if the investor wants to get his investment back before the bond matures, he can sell it to another investor, in the secondary market.

The price of a bond in the secondary market depends on several factors, including the financial condition of the issuer, prevailing interest rates, and supply and demand.

Broker.

A broker is an intermediary who is responsible for executing orders to buy and sell financial assets placed with him by his clients. The broker may be an individual or a firm.

The broker charges a commission for each transaction it executes on behalf of its clients, whether buying or selling, and must comply with a number of legal and regulatory requirements in order to conduct its business.

Stock brokers operate only in the stock market, but a broker may operate in other financial markets, such as foreign exchange, commodities or cryptocurrencies.

Call / Purchase Option.

A call is a contract that gives the buyer the right to buy an asset at a fixed price in the future.

For this right, the buyer pays an amount called a premium to the seller of the option.

The seller is obligated to sell the asset if the buyer exercises the option.

Cartel.

An agreement, illegal in most jurisdictions, among several similar companies to avoid competition with each other and to regulate production, sales and prices in a particular geographic or commercial area.

Cash Flow.

Cash flow is the difference between a company's income and expenses in a given period.

More simply, it is the ability of a company to generate cash after paying expenses in a specified period.

Cash flow shows the company's ability to generate cash and pay its obligations.

CBDC.

Central Bank Digital Currency.

A type of fiat currency equivalent to physical cash such as banknotes and coins, but in digital format, similar to cryptocurrencies, but centralized. Like its physical cash equivalent, as a fiat currency it is not backed by anything other than legal tender. See the term: fiat

Central Bank.

The central bank is the institution that issues and manages legal tender and performs the function of banker to the commercial banks.

It also controls the monetary system, by controlling the issue of money, and the credit system, by controlling interest rates.

In mixed economies or those with heavy government intervention, it also controls the foreign exchange market, controlling the exchange rate with other foreign currencies.

In an ideal capitalist system, the exchange rate between currencies should fluctuate freely according to the supply and demand of each currency.

However, there are agreements between central banks called currency swaps*, which consist of a temporary exchange of currencies between two central banks with a commitment to return them at a future date and at a fixed exchange rate.

There is also a tacit agreement between the main central banks to guarantee convertibility between a small group of currencies called convertible currencies.

These are: the Euro, the US Dollar, the Pound Sterling, the Japanese Yen and the Swiss Franc.

It is common for the central banks of these currencies to act in concert in the event of international exchange rate tensions to avoid too sharp fluctuations, buying or selling currencies as a group to alleviate specific problems.

The main functions of a central bank are, to act as the bank of the state, and control the issue of currency.

Receive deposits from commercial banks and make loans to commercial banks and governments.

To manage monetary policy and control a country's inflation.

They are also responsible for making currency transfers with other countries in the world and regulating and auditing the activities of commercial banks in their area.

CFTC

Commodity Futures Trading Commission (CFTC).

A U.S. agency that oversees and regulates the trading of futures and options contracts on commodities, raw materials, currencies, indices and other assets such as derivatives, futures, options and swaps.

Commodity.

In the plural, commodities are those generic or basic products that vary little in price, appearance, or use, such as raw materials like oil, timber, grain, or precious metals.

They are tangible materials that can be traded, bought, or sold without further processing.

Creditor / Debtor.

These are the two parties to a financial transaction.
A creditor is the one who has the right to claim a debt from his debtor.
A debtor is one who has the obligation to pay a debt to its creditor.

Crypto-asset

A crypto-asset is a type of digital asset, or token, based on cryptography (a branch of mathematics) and blockchain, that has a certain market value by utility or demand and can generate income by selling it or exchanging it for goods or services.

Cryptocurrency.

It is a crypto-asset, but which, in addition to basing its value on a possible utility and/or demand, meets the characteristics that define money.

In this author's opinion, only bitcoin is a cryptocurrency, all other "cryptocurrencies" called alt-coins or alternative currencies are actually tokens or crypto-assets.

Cryptography.

It is a branch of mathematics that deals with the techniques of encrypting and decrypting, or encoding and decoding, information. Cryptography is based on the mathematical theory of numbers.

Currency.

Colloquially, they are used interchangeably, but currency is the physical unit or unit of account, and foreign currency refers to the generic name of a foreign country's monetary units.
The official name of China's currency is the renminbi, but its basic unit is the yuan.

Dividends.

Dividends are the portion of earnings that a company distributes to its shareholders. Dividends are the primary way in which shareholders are compensated as owners of a company.

Dow Jones (Stock Index)

Usually refers to: Dow Jones Industrial Average, which is a stock market index consisting of the 30 companies with the largest market capitalization on the New York Stock Exchange, excluding transportation and utility companies.

There are other specific indexes with the same name:
Dow Jones Industrial Average (DJIA), mentioned above.
Dow Jones Utility Average (DJUA): This reflects the securities of the 15 largest companies in markets such as gas and electricity.
Dow Jones Transportation Average (DJTA) Includes the 20 largest transportation and distribution companies.

Dow Jones Composite Average (DJCA) Index that measures the performance of the shares of 65 member companies of any of the above three main indexes.

Economy / Economics (Social science)

Economics is the social science that studies the laws that govern the production, distribution, and consumption of goods and services in the most efficient way to satisfy human needs.

Equity.

A company's equity, commonly referred to as stockholders' equity, is the amount of money that would be returned to stockholders if all of the company's assets were liquidated and all of the company's debts were repaid.

Equity financing allows the company to raise sufficient funds without borrowing or incurring debt.

Equity financing involves the sale of stock in the company. A portion of the company's ownership is given to investors in exchange for cash.

ETF

From "Exchange-Traded Fund".

An ETF is a financial instrument that is traded on an exchange and is designed to replicate the performance of a stock market index, a commodity, or a specific market sector.

In a mutual fund, an investor usually cannot withdraw his participation until a predefined date, on the contrary, ETFs are investment funds that are divided into units, or "shares".

Investors can buy and sell ETF shares on the stock exchange just like shares.

EURIBOR / LIBOR

Euro Interbank Offered Rate is the reference interest rate used in the European interbank market.

The Euribor is calculated from the average of the interest rates reported by the banks in the sample. It is calculated daily for different maturities, such as 1 week, 1 month, 3 months, 6 months and 1 year.

LIBOR is similar to Euribor: London InterBank Offered Rate (LIBOR) is the daily bank rate based on the rates at which UK banks lend money to each other in the wholesale interbank market.

Note that banks "declare" the interest rates they charge other banks, but are not actually required to document that they actually charge the declared rates.

This detail has on several occasions allowed large banks to falsify the interbank interest rate and receive convictions, but with rather light economic sanctions.

Exchange Rate (Foreign Exchange).

The price of one currency expressed in terms of another currency, i.e., the number of units of one currency required to obtain one unit of another currency.

Exchange rates between currencies should be freely determined by the market according to supply and demand, but governments and central banks try to intervene to change the exchange rate of their currency according to their interests. This usually has negative and counterproductive effects.

Fiat Money / Fiduciary Currency.

From the Latin "Let's make it".

A currency that represents a value that it does not actually have.

All current national currencies are fiat, with the exception of Gold and Bitcoin.

Fiat money is money that has no intrinsic value, nor is it backed by the precious metal reserves of its issuer; its value exists because the law says it has that value.

Financial Arbitrage.

A financial strategy that involves taking advantage of the difference in price between different markets for the same financial asset to gain an economic advantage.
If a company's stock is quoted at different prices in two markets, an investor can buy stock in the market where the price is lower and sell it in the market where the price is higher; this price difference is the profit.
This type of operation is carried out automatically by computer systems with the so-called high frequency trading, in operations that can be carried out in milliseconds.
The automatic arbitrage makes the price differences of the same asset tend to quote the same price, even if they are traded in different markets, quickly.

Financial Derivative.

A financial derivative is a financial product whose value depends on the value of another asset, called the underlying.

More simply put, they are bets based on the price of another asset.

An example of a financial derivative is a contract for difference (CFD). A CFD is a contract where the investor and the broker exchange the difference in the price of a particular underlying asset. For example, if you buy a CFD on Apple stock and the stock price goes up, the broker pays you the difference. If it goes down, you pay the broker.

Financial indicator.

A financial indicator is a numerical data point that provides information about a variable used to measure, for example, liquidity, solvency, debt, profitability, or simply the price of an asset over a period of time.

There are many types of indicators, but there are two broad categories: leading indicators, which make it possible to predict a situation before it occurs, and lagging indicators, which show past performance.

Numerical data can be used to create a graph.

Visualizing data through graphs helps to identify patterns, trends, relationships, and data structures.

Financial Record.

A financial record is a document that details a company's financial transactions, such as a receipt, bank statement or invoice, bank statements, payment vouchers, contracts, etc.

Financial records are important because they provide evidence of a company's business activities and serve as the basis for financial accounting.

Fintech.

Acronym for Financial Technology. It is a term that refers to the application of information and communication technologies in the financial industry, with the aim of improving and optimizing financial services. Fintech companies use technologies such as artificial intelligence, big data, blockchain, and automation to provide more efficient, convenient, and personalized financial solutions.

Fintech companies offer a wide range of products and services, ranging from mobile banking apps, electronic payments, online lending, investment management, insurance, to accounting and corporate finance solutions.

Fintech companies have emerged as an alternative to traditional financial services and have been able to provide more efficient and cost-effective cross-border services than banks.

Fixed Income / Variable Income. (Equities).

Fixed income is a type of investment that includes all financial assets where the issuer is obligated to make payments in a predetermined amount and period of time. In other words, the issuer guarantees the return of the invested capital and a certain predetermined profitability.

Fixed income securities can be sold on the secondary market without waiting for them to mature, but supply and demand affect their price. Therefore, a fixed income security has a "fixed" return only if the security is held to maturity.

An example of a fixed income investment is bonds or debt securities issued by governments or corporations to finance their activities.

Variable income is a type of investment that consists of buying financial assets whose profitability is not guaranteed or known in advance. Variable income implies a higher risk than fixed income, but it also offers the possibility of higher profits if the value of the assets increases in the market. The main equity instruments are stocks or equity securities.

Forex.

Also, FX, is an abbreviation for Foreign Exchange. Foreign exchange takes place when one country's currency is exchanged for another country's currency. Forex is the largest financial market in the world, trading some $5 trillion daily.

GDP (Gross Domestic Product.)

Gross domestic product is the value of all final goods and services produced in a country or region during a period of time, usually 1 year.

Government (Public) Debt.

Public debt, or sovereign debt, is the total amount of debt owed by a government to individuals, institutions or other governments.

A way of obtaining financial resources by states that spend more than they take in. Usually by issuing securities or bonds.

High Yield Bond.

Also known as junk bonds. A high yield bond is a fixed income bond that offers a high rate of return but with a high risk of default.

The offer of high-yield bonds is due to the risk that the issuer may not be able to pay the interest or the principal when the bond matures or the interest is due.

The issuers of these bonds are companies or governments with low credit ratings, below investment grade.

However, a good credit rating is no guarantee of the issuer's solvency

Inflation.

The loss of purchasing power of money.

Inflation is not the general increase in prices.

The generalized rise in prices is the result, not the cause, and is always a monetary event driven by the issuance of money.

The more money in circulation for the same quantity of goods or services, the lower the value of money, so more money is needed to buy the same goods or services.

Initial Public Offer.

An Initial Public Offer (IPO) is the selling of securities to the public in the primary market. It is the largest source of funds with long or indefinite maturity for the company.

The initial public offering (IPO) of a company's shares is a process that is regulated by law and subject to the scrutiny of the relevant financial authorities.

Interest / Negative Interest.

In economics and finance, interest is the additional amount paid or charged for the use of borrowed or invested money over a given period of time. It is essentially the cost of using money and is usually expressed as a percentage of the amount borrowed or invested.

Negative interest: A euphemistic term used to describe an anomalous and aberrant situation in which borrowers (who have borrowed money) charge lenders (who make the loan) interest for the use of the borrowed money instead of paying interest on the loan.

This means that the lender receives less money than originally lent, instead of receiving the principal plus an additional amount as interest.

Negative interest rates are very bad for savers, who lose money instead of earning interest on their savings. It is also detrimental to financial institutions, which rely on interest income to keep their businesses profitable. In general, negative interest rates are an anomalous phenomenon and are generally considered a last resort in economic policy.

The European Central Bank (ECB) has maintained negative interest rates since June 2014, when it lowered its deposit rate to -0.10%. It then cut the deposit rate further to -0.50% in September 2019, and kept it negative until July 2022.

Interest Rates (from a Central Bank)

A central bank's interest rate is an important monetary policy tool. If a central bank wants to stimulate economic growth, it can lower the interest rate, which makes borrowing cheaper and encourages spending and investment.

If the central bank wants to cool the economy and control inflation, it can raise the interest rate, which makes borrowing more expensive and discourages spending and investment, and by restricting credit it slows the creation of money generated by commercial bank credit.

This process is discussed in Chapter 2.

Central bank interest rates also affect the value of the national currency. When a central bank raises its interest rate, it makes its currency more attractive to foreign investors because they can earn a higher return on their investments in that currency.

When commercial banks deposit with their central bank the money they have not yet lent to their customers, the central bank pays them the interest rate set by the central bank.

The interest rates set by central banks, not by the market, are the base price of money that affects all other interest rates.

Por For example, mortgage interest rates are based on the EURIBOR interbank rate, which in turn is based on the European Central Bank's base rate.

To give an example:

If the European Central Bank sets a rate of 3%, the banks will set a higher rate, let's say 4%, which is their profit, when they lend to other banks, which is set by Euribor, and the mortgages will again have the interest rate set by Euribor plus the difference, which is the bank's profit. Continuing with the example, it could be 5%.

If the central bank lowers interest rates to 2%, the Euribor would probably follow this fall to 3% and the variable rate mortgages would fall to 4%.

In this way, the interest rates set by the central banks are the base price on which the market then sets all other interest rates applied in the financial market.

Investment Fund.

A form of investment that pools money from several investors to invest in financial assets such as stocks, bonds, real estate, or other securities with the goal of earning a profit.

Mutual funds are managed by professional managers who make investment decisions on behalf of investors.

When an investor invests in a fund, he or she buys a pro rata share of the fund. Each share has a net asset value, which is calculated daily based on the value of the fund's underlying assets. At the end of each liquidation period, the fund's gains or losses are shared proportionately among the investors.

ISIN (Code)

The ISIN code (International Securities Identification Number) is developed in the international standard ISO 6166 and is used to identify securities. It is a code that uniquely identifies a security on an international level and is used by all financial markets worldwide that have incorporated it into their settlement and custody processes.

Leverage.

A system of financing the purchase of assets with borrowed money. For example, an investor may invest his capital in a financial asset, but add to his capital an amount borrowed from a company.

This system has a peculiarity that is necessary to understand, as it is usually the mechanism that triggers most financial disasters.
In a x10 leverage, the investor contributes 1 part and the entity providing the leverage contributes 10 times the investor's initial capital, in exchange, of course, for a percentage of interest that the investor must pay.

This capital is used to buy a financial asset, for example a number of shares; if the value of these shares rises, the investor can sell them with a profit of x10 times his capital and thus pay the interest on the temporary loan he used to buy the shares.
The danger comes when the value of the shares falls, in this case the entity that lent the investor x10 the capital, which monitors the price of these shares, observes that the loss of value of the shares purchased on credit is approaching the real capital contributed by the investor, then warns, if there is time, the investor to add more capital to maintain his investment, this notice is called margin call, or call to maintain the margin of safety.

If the investor is unwilling or unable to provide more capital, then the lender, before the loss affects the investor's loan, executes the sale of the shares, which is called liquidation, with the investor losing all of his capital, and if the process has been carried out correctly, the lender will lose nothing.

Sometimes the financial markets can fluctuate so rapidly that the company that lent the leveraged capital has literally no time to liquidate, or if it does liquidate, it suffers a loss.
In April 2021, several large banks, and in particular the Swiss bank Credit Suisse, lost 4 billion as the entity that provided financing to the Archegos fund.

This fund lost 10 billion in 48 hours. Not being able to provide more capital, the companies that financed the investment of Archegos Capital liquidated their assets of more than 30 billion, incurring terrible losses, since the sale of such an amount of shares accelerates the price decline.

This type of cases is not frequent, usually the entities that provide the financing of leverage in the financial markets usually repay the borrowed capital before it is lost, the one who always loses all his capital is the leveraged investor whose leveraged asset is liquidated.

Leverage is the norm in financial markets, and it generates huge profits in a bull market, but terrible losses in a bear market.

A large leveraged financial operation that goes wrong can drag a credit institution into insolvency, which in turn affects other institutions, as the liquidations accelerate price declines in the stock market, which in turn affect other investors leveraged with that or other institutions, creating a downward spiral.

Liquidity.

The ease and or speed with which an asset can be bought or sold without significantly affecting its price.

Generally, securities issued by the U.S. government are considered the most liquid assets in the economy, because there are always many buyers and sellers and sales and purchases can be very quick.

At the other extreme are real estate with very little liquidity, because there may be few buyers interested in a given real estate property, and these sales and purchases require more time to be formalized.

Margin Call.

A request by a broker or dealer for an investor to contribute more capital to his or her margin account because the value of the assets held in the account has fallen below the minimum margin required by the exchange. Margin is the money an investor lends through his or her broker to invest in financial assets.

If the investor fails to comply with the Margin Call request, the broker has the right to close out the investor's positions to recover the borrowed money. Forced liquidation can result in large losses for the investor.

mBridge.

The Bank for International Settlements (BIS or central bank of central banks) mBridge project is an initiative to explore and assess the potential of blockchain technology and cryptocurrencies in financial markets.

The mBridge project focuses specifically on the use of blockchain technology for the settlement of cross-border interbank transactions, which could offer significant advantages in terms of efficiency, speed and cost compared to traditional settlement methods.

The mBridge project is being developed by the Technology Innovation Hub of the Bank for International Settlements.

Monetary Mass. M1, M2, M3.

Money supply is the total amount of money in circulation in an economy. It is commonly divided into three groups: M1, M2 and M3.

M1: This is the most liquid money in circulation, i.e. cash, notes and coins in the hands of the public and bank demand deposits, or those that can be withdrawn at any time.

M2: Includes everything that makes up M1, plus time deposits, money market mutual funds or other short-term funds.

M3: Money supply M3 is the broadest measure of money supply because it includes everything in M2, plus long-term deposits and other financial instruments such as government bonds and corporate debt, but long-term.

That is, assets that take much longer to be converted into cash, i.e., less liquid assets.

M3 is useful for analyzing the long-term money supply and its impact on the overall economy.

Money.

Any medium of exchange generally accepted by a society for buying and selling goods and services.
While it must have certain characteristics such as:
Acceptability, Divisibility, Interchangeability, Unit of Account, Reserve of value, Scarcity, Portability, Durability, and Fungibility.

Mortgage.

A long-term loan used to purchase real estate, such as a house, apartment or land. The mortgage is used to finance the purchase of the property and is secured by the property itself. This means that the property is the collateral for the loan; if the borrower defaults on the agreed payments, the lender can take possession of the property to recover its investment.

Each monthly payment includes a portion of the loan principal and interest due on the outstanding principal, which means that the interest portion of the monthly payment is higher at the beginning of the loan and decreases as the loan principal is amortized.

Mortgages can be fixed rate or variable rate mortgages. In Europe, the 1-year Euribor is used as a reference.

For variable rate mortgages, the lending bank will mark a spread over the Euribor. For example, 1% over the Euribor index and the rates are revised every 6 months according to this index. If the Euribor is at 4%, the interest rate of the mortgage will be 5%.

It is very important to understand that the interest paid is always on the capital still to be paid, so the longer the duration, the more interest will be paid, even if the installments are a little lower.

Here is an example to help you understand **in numbers** what the interest rates on a typical mortgage loan mean.

Capital to be financed: 200.000 €.

Term: 30 years.

Fixed interest rate for the example: 5.5%.

Monthly payment: 1.135,58 €.

Total amount paid at the end (30 years): 408.808,80 €.

In other words, for the example data, the mortgagor will have paid more than twice the capital he financed.

NASDAQ.

An acronym for National Association of Securities Dealers Automated Quotations, a U.S. electronic stock exchange where shares of technology and related companies are traded.

The NASDAQ is divided into two main markets: the NASDAQ Composite and the NASDAQ-100.

The NASDAQ Composite is a market index that includes all companies listed on the NASDAQ, while the NASDAQ-100 is a market index that includes the 100 largest and most actively traded companies on the NASDAQ.

Founded in 1971, NASDAQ was the world's first electronic stock exchange.

Offshore Financial Services.

Offshore financial services refer to financial products and services that are offered by financial institutions based in countries or jurisdictions that have lower taxes, fewer regulations, and greater financial privacy than the customer's home country.

These services may include banking, investment management, insurance, and other financial products that are offered to individuals, corporations, or institutional investors.

The term "offshore" generally refers to locations that are outside of the customer's home country, although some jurisdictions may be located onshore but offer similar tax and regulatory benefits.

Companies and individuals who use offshore financial services often seek to reduce their tax burden or protect their assets from confiscation or litigation. However, the use of offshore financial services has also been criticized for facilitating tax evasion and money laundering.

Overton. The Overton Window.

The Overton Window is a political theory that describes how social opinion can change in several stages (or a time window) so that an idea that is initially totally unacceptable can eventually and gradually be introduced and accepted by society.

This is one of the most important and widely used mechanisms of political power, nowadays also called social engineering, to impose initially unacceptable laws and norms, usually to restrict freedom, increase control and taxes.

Ponzi Scheme (Ponzi Fraud)

A Ponzi scheme is a type of investment fraud in which returns are paid to earlier investors using the capital contributed by newer investors, rather than from any actual profits generated by the investment. The scheme is named after Charles Ponzi, who became notorious for using this method to defraud investors in the early 20th century.

In a Ponzi scheme, the promoter of the scheme promises high returns to investors, often using complex and seemingly legitimate investment strategies. The promoter may use fake or misleading financial statements, or may simply lie about the returns generated by the investment.

As more investors are brought into the scheme, the promoter uses their money to pay off earlier investors, creating the illusion of profitable returns. However, eventually the scheme will collapse, either because the promoter can no longer attract enough new investors to pay off the earlier ones, or because too many investors try to cash out at once and there isn't enough money to cover their withdrawals.

Ponzi schemes are illegal in most countries, and participants can face serious legal and financial consequences if caught. It's important for investors to be wary of investment opportunities that seem too good to be true and to do their due diligence before investing.

Primary Market / Secondary Market.

The primary market is where new securities or assets are issued and sold to the public to raise capital.

The secondary market is where investors buy and sell securities that have already been issued in the primary market.

In this market, investors buy and sell securities among themselves without the direct involvement of the issuer.

Profitability.

This is the quality of generating profits or earnings and is expressed as a percentage or the ratio of the profits generated to the capital invested.

Proof of Work. "PoW" (Bitcoin Network)

Proof of Work is a consensus mechanism that uses the processing power of miners to secure the Bitcoin network and guarantee the validity of transactions. While effective, it consumes a lot of computing power and therefore a lot of energy.

Proof of work secures the Bitcoin network by making it very difficult and expensive for an attacker to alter or forge transactions or blocks. To do so, the attacker would need to have more computing power than the other miners, which would require a large investment of energy and money. In addition, PoW incentivizes miners to follow the rules and maintain the integrity of the network by rewarding them in BTC for doing so.

Quantitative Easing "QE"/ Quantitative Tightening. "QT"

Quantitative Easing (QE) is a form of expansionary monetary policy used by central banks to increase the money supply and stimulate the economy. In QE, the central bank buys government bonds and other financial instruments, such as mortgage-backed securities, with electronically created new money.

Quantitative Tightening (QT) is a contractionary monetary policy tool used by central banks to reduce the amount of liquidity or money in the economy. QT is the opposite of Quantitative Easing (QE). The central bank implements QT by selling or letting government bonds mature and removing them from its cash balance. The goal is to raise interest rates, discourage lending and investment, and control inflation.

Rating.

The rating or financial rating is a qualification that indicates the credit risk of a company, country or financial product. The rating is provided by credit rating agencies, which are private entities that evaluate the solvency and payment capacity of debt issuers.

The rating is expressed by a series of letters and symbols ranging from AAA (highest credit quality) to D (default).

Russel 2000.

The Russell 2000 is a stock market index that measures the performance of approximately 2,000 small-cap companies in the United States. It is often used as a benchmark for small-cap stocks or as an indicator of the health of the broader U.S. stock market.

El The Russell 2000 is composed of smaller companies with market capitalizations ranging from approximately $300 million to $2 billion.

S&P500.

It is a stock market index that reflects the performance of the 500 largest and most important companies in the U.S. stock market. It is one of the most widely used indexes in the financial world and is considered a representative measure of the performance of the U.S. stock market.

The S&P 500 is a market-capitalization-weighted measure, which means that larger companies have a greater weight in the index than smaller companies.

SEC.

The Securities and Exchange Commission. An independent U.S. federal agency responsible for protecting investors and maintaining the integrity of the U.S. securities market.

The SEC's responsibilities include:

Protecting investors, regulating the securities market, and promoting transparency.

The SEC also has the authority to enforce the federal securities laws and can bring legal action against individuals and companies that violate these laws.

Security.

In financial terminology, the term "security" refers to a tradable financial asset that holds some type of monetary value. This includes stocks, bonds, options, futures, and other derivatives. A security can represent ownership in a company (in the case of stocks) or a creditor relationship with a company or government entity (in the case of bonds).

Securities are traded on financial markets and can be bought and sold by investors with the expectation of generating a return on their investment.

The term "security" is a legal term that is often used in regulatory and compliance contexts as well

Shares.

A share is a portion of a company's capital that can be bought and sold on the stock exchange.

Essentially, it is one of the forms of financing a company; when a company needs capital or financing to conduct its business, it sells securities that represent equal portions of that capital, and those portions or securities or shares can be bought and sold on a regulated market called the stock exchange.

Shareholders.

The owners of the shares who have rights to the company and its profits.

Share - Stock market value.

The terms "share" and "stock" are often used interchangeably, but technically they have slightly different meanings.

A share refers to a single unit of ownership in a company. If a company is divided into multiple units of ownership, each of those units is called a share. These shares are issued by the company to raise capital, and shareholders who own these shares are entitled to a share of the company's profits, as well as the right to vote on certain matters.

On the other hand, stock refers to the total ownership units in a company represented by shares. Thus, "stock" is a more general term that includes all shares issued by a company.

In practice, the terms "share" and "stock" are often used interchangeably to refer to ownership interests in a company. However, in certain contexts, such as legal documents or financial statements, the distinction between the two terms can be important.

Stock market value is calculated by multiplying the current price of a share, or the price at a given time, by the total number of shares of that company.

Sell short. Short selling.

A "short" in the stock market is an investment technique that allows investors to bet on the decline of a security or index. This technique is used to make a profit when the stock price falls and is known as "short selling" or "short position".

It works as follows.

If an investor believes that a security or stock will go down in price, he can borrow a certain number of those shares, paying an amount, let's say as a "rent" or loan, to the owner, with the obligation to return them at the expiration of the "short" contract.

As soon as the investor receives the shares, he sells them and waits for the price to fall.

When the price has fallen, he buys them back at a lower price and returns them to the owner who lent them to him.

The profit is the percentage drop minus the amount he had to pay for the "rent" or loan.

Short's technique is risky and complex and is usually done with a rollover, which increases the risk exponentially. The worst scenario for a short is that the shares that were expected to go down start to go up, so the short seller has to buy them as soon as possible because he will be forced to give them back and now he has to buy them more expensive.

If a stock has many short sellers, they can force the stock to go down in price, but if the opposite happens and the stock starts to go up, all the short sellers will rush to buy as soon as possible so that they can return the shares they borrowed to short, since the increase in price will cause them losses because they will have to buy them back more expensively.

If many short sellers rush to buy the shares to be returned, it will cause an accelerated rise in price, creating a chain reaction that will trap other short sellers who will also be forced to buy to mitigate the losses.

In general, these types of events are extremely abrupt and, as mentioned, are usually leveraged, which usually results in forced liquidations of positions with huge losses for the short sellers.

These market events are known as "short squeezes".

Solvency.

Solvency refers to the ability of a company or individual to meet its long-term financial obligations, i.e., its ability to pay all outstanding debts in the future.

Solvency should not be confused with liquidity, which refers to the ability of a company or individual to meet its short-term financial obligations, i.e., to pay its immediate debts.

Spread.

The difference between two prices, interest rates or yields on different financial instruments.

In the foreign exchange market, the spread is the difference between the bid and ask price of a currency pair, where the spread represents the broker's profit.

In the bond market, the spread is the difference between the yield on one bond and the yield on another bond with a similar credit rating.

Stablecoin.

A stablecoin is a type of cryptocurrency that is tied to another asset, such as a fiat currency.

For example, one unit of a stablecoin may be equal to one U.S. dollar.

The issuing company must hold one unit of the linked currency as backing for each unit of cryptocurrency issued.

Some of the best known are USDT or Theter, and USDC from Circle.

Stock Exchange.

The stock exchange is a market or institution where stocks, bonds, and other financial instruments that represent the value of a company or debt are bought and sold.

The exchange allows investors to trade these instruments for the purpose of making profits or financing businesses.

The first official stock exchange was established in 1602 in Amsterdam by the Dutch East India Company, which was the first to issue shares to the public, marking a financial breakthrough by dividing into equal parts (shares) the capital needed to finance a company that would also share its profits (dividends) in proportion to the number of shares owned by each shareholder.

Until then, business activities usually required a financier who provided a large amount of capital and was the sole owner of the company and the sole recipient of any profits.

By dividing capital into many smaller pieces, companies could raise capital from many investors.

This development led to a great economic boom that spurred trade and, later, the Industrial Revolution.

Supply and demand.

These are the two basic concepts that explain how markets work, where supply is the amount of a good or service that producers are willing to sell at a given price, and demand is the amount of a good or service that consumers are willing to buy at a given price.

If supply is greater than demand, prices will tend to fall because sellers will have to compete with each other by lowering prices to attract buyers; on the other hand, if demand is greater than supply, buyers will have to compete with each other by offering a higher price to buy the goods or services offered, so the price will tend to rise.

Swap.

A swap is a financial contract in which two parties agree to exchange future cash flows according to agreed-upon terms.

Swaps can be interest rate swaps, currency swaps, or swaps on other financial assets.

For example, a company that has a fixed interest rate on a loan may agree to exchange cash flows with another company that has a floating interest rate on a similar loan.

This allows the company to convert its fixed interest rate to a variable interest rate, which can provide greater financial flexibility and reduce interest rate risk.

Another common type of swap is a currency swap.

For example, an American company may need euros and a European company may need dollars for their respective operations.

Instead of using a currency swap, they could agree to a swap, which is an agreement for a fixed period of time in which the European company sends Euros to the American company and the American company sends Dollars to the European company, according to the exchange rate fixed at the time the swap is entered into, plus an interest rate that attempts to anticipate possible changes in the euro/dollar exchange rate.

SWIFT.

Society for Worldwide Interbank Financial Telecommunications.

It is a global financial messaging network used by banks and other financial institutions to exchange information and conduct financial transactions in a secure and reliable manner.

The SWIFT network is owned by its members and managed by the SWIFT Cooperative, headquartered in Belgium.

Token.

They are digital assets that represent a specific value or asset and are used in the cryptocurrency and blockchain world for various purposes, such as representing real assets, crowdfunding and speculation.

Tokens differ from bitcoin in that they are designed to represent a specific value rather than being used as a form of payment.

Trust (Company) / Trustee.

A trust is a legal agreement in which an individual or organization (the trustor or settlor) transfers assets to a trustee. The trustee is then responsible for managing those assets for the benefit of the trust's beneficiaries in accordance with the terms of the trust agreement.
A trustee is an individual or organization responsible for managing the assets placed in a trust. The trustee performs this role on behalf of a grantor, the person who created and funded the trust.

It is a contract by which a person, called the grantor (or trustor or settlor), transfers certain assets for a specific lawful purpose and entrusts the realization of that purpose to a trust institution which, at a certain time or when the condition imposed by the grantor of the assets is fulfilled, must deliver to the beneficiary or trustee the fruits or products generated by the activity.

The assets transferred to the trust are not at the commercial risk of the settlor (the one who transfers the ownership of the assets) or of the trustee (the owner of the trust assets at the end of the term of the contract), since the assets that are the subject of the trust cannot be pursued by the creditors of either of them, nor can they be affected by the bankruptcy of both or one of them.

The trustee (the one who administers the assigned property) may, by extension, refer to the person or entity that provides the service to the settlor (the one who assigns the property).

VIX. (Index)

The VIX (CBOE Volatility Index) is an indicator of the implied volatility of put and call options on the S&P 500 Index, which is used to measure market expectations of future equity market volatility.

The VIX Index is considered a measure of market "fear" or "anxiety" and is commonly used as a risk management tool for investors.

Volatility.

Stock market volatility refers to the measure of the magnitude and frequency of changes in the price of a security, index or market.

In other words, volatility is a statistical measure of the number and magnitude of fluctuations that a financial asset experiences in a given period of time.

However, the term volatility is often used colloquially, beyond its precise meaning, to describe uncertainty about asset prices and, more frequently, to emphasize potential price declines.

Yield.

Refers to the profit, if the return is positive, or loss, if the return is negative, earned on an investment, expressed as a percentage of the capital invested.

High-yield bonds are a euphemism for junk bonds, which are bonds issued by institutions with poor credit ratings and a high risk of default. These bonds usually offer a high rate of interest. However, there is a high risk of default.